HOW TO TAP YOUR HIDDEN TREASURE

Your personal guide to a life of fulfillment

The page is intentionally left blank

HOW TO TAP YOUR HIDDEN TREASURE

Your personal guide to a life of fulfillment

Job Lazarus Okello
The Legend of Inspiration

PENWALL MEDIA LIMITED

How to tap your hidden treasure.
Copyright © 2018 by Job Lazarus Okello.

Published by Penwall Media Limited
P.O. Box 50062, Luzira, Kampala, Uganda
Visit our website at www.penwallmedia.com
E-mail: info@penwallmedia.com

Printed in Uganda

ISBN 978-9970-9826-0-8

"A masterpiece that tremendously enlightens the reader's life. It's a phenomenal documentation of Job's inspirational traits. You will find it very hard to put the book down once you start reading it."

-Kasakye Andrew Philip, Mechanical Technician, Department of Mechanical Engineering, Makerere University

"The book is inspiring beyond the reader's utmost imagination; it delivers the answers to many life's questions. I warmly recommend it to everybody."

-Monsignor Sebestian Newman Odong, Spiritual Director, Sacred Heart Seminary, Lacor; former Episcopal Vicar-Gulu Vicariate, Gulu Archdiocese

"An eye-opener to the realities of life. In it, Job prudently reveals to the world how gifted he is. Whoever reads the book will never waste or permit anyone to waste their life in any way."

-Simon Peter Okello, Founder and Executive Director, Northern Uganda Transparency and Accountability Forum (NUTAFO); Founder and Director, Origin Microfinance

Other books by Job Lazarus Okello

Light at the end of the tunnel

Sailing through the storms of life

You can make it

Cross before crown

DEDICATION

This book is warmly dedicated to
Mrs. Okumu Anna, *former head teacher,*
St. Mary's College, Lacor, for nurturing me into
what I have become. Truly, you are more than
a mentor to me.

ACKNOWLEDGEMENTS

It takes a great team of committed people to produce a life-transforming book. It is courteous to acknowledge the people who make up such a team for their various contributions.

In a special way, I appreciate Charlotte Akello, for editing the book and providing outstanding suggestions based on her extensive literature experience.

With great honor, I thank Gerald Oyeki of Penwall Media Limited, a great literary agent, who provided precious guidance and encouragement and shared great ideas with me at every stage of production of this book.

Heartfelt appreciation is expressed to Etwalu Emmanuel Brian, Wokorach Geoffrey, Onencan Stephen, Magere David, Mrs. Okumu Anna, Kica Omol Dan, Amarorwot Vicky, Mutebi Julius and Amolo Fiona, who contributed financially towards the production of the book.

With great love and honor, I thank Mrs. Okumu Anna for offering valuable encouragement throughout the writing and production of this book.

Sincere gratitude is expressed to Amarorwot Vicky for providing tremendous assistance that made it possible for me to complete the book.

I am grateful to my pretty little sister, Acaa Mary, the chief supporter of this project, for always praying for me to succeed in all my endeavors.

I am greatly indebted to my precious father John Ongom Obina and glorious mother Florence Auma, who taught me in my childhood to set out to transform the world.

I am enormously appreciative to Professor Nyeko Pen-Mogi Jack Howard, Associate Professor Omona Julius, Monsignor Sebastian Newman Odong, Mrs. Okumu Anna, Komakech John Bosco, Kasakye Andrew Philip, Simon Peter Okello and Charlotte Akello, for reviewing the book.

Finally, to all those who supported this project yet whose names are not mentioned here, I am truly grateful.

May the ever-good Lord reward you all immensely.

Contents

INTRODUCTION

Hidden inside everyone is a great treasure. Unfortunately for most people, it is unexploited. Either they do not know how to tap it or are not even aware of its existence.

How to tap your hidden treasure delivers the recipes for realizing your treasure and ultimately exploiting it. It was written to serve as your personal guide to an improved life. To get the most out of this book, read it thoroughly and apply the lessons in your daily life. Your life will continuously improve. Do not rush to finish the book; read it carefully so that you grasp the principles laid out in it.

I advise you to make your personal summary of each of the chapters of the book as you read it. This will help you to master the concepts in the book. Very important to note and keep in mind is that this is a life-transforming book. Therefore, as you read it and apply its lessons, your life will immensely get transformed and the results will be evident.

You may read the book with someone or in groups and discuss it with others so as to widen your understanding of its concepts. While you do that, your focus should be on how you can apply the concepts and how you want your life to improve thereafter. This book was written for you, to better your life. Therefore, own and utilize it ultimately. The inspirations in the book will improve the way you perceive life. Kindly recommend the book to a friend or put a copy in their hands so that they too can read it and get transformed. This book will surely help you to discover and fully tap your hidden treasure so that you fulfill your life's purpose.

CHAPTER ONE
LET OUT THE GREAT TREASURE INSIDE YOU

Do you think you are living your best life right now? Do you view the life which you are living right now as your ultimate? Do you think you have done all that you could ever do? If you answered 'yes' to even only one of the above questions, then you are absolutely wrong. Inside you still lie great untapped abilities. In other words, you can do more than what you have done and accomplish more than what you have accomplished. What you have done is only a fraction of what you were created to do. There is a lot more you can still do than you can ever imagine.

Therefore, never settle for what you have already achieved; be hungry for more. Successful people are never satisfied with their achievements. To achieve more, you should be hungry for more. Maybe you have been concentrating on only one area or just a few areas of your life leaving the rest untouched. With this, therefore, to say that you are living at the peak of your life right now is a terrible claim; you would only be deceiving yourself. A great personality still lies inside you whom you have to discover and thereafter let out. No one can ever do that for you; it is entirely your responsibility to do it.

Maybe a very powerful entrepreneur is hidden inside you, let out the entrepreneur. Or perhaps an amazing teacher is hidden inside you-one who can greatly transform the world, let out this teacher. You may wrongly think that you have exhausted all your abilities when inside you is still hidden a life-transforming personality; let out this personality. You could be 80 years old and wrongly thinking that there is nothing more you that can still achieve when there is an industrialist hidden inside you; the next Henry Ford could be hidden inside you, let out the industrialist.

You may be a scientist and comfortable with what you have done when the next Sir Isaac Newton is hidden inside you-let out the powerful scientist. Are you an engineer? Do you think that is all you can be? If you answered 'yes', then you are wrong! Inside you could be hidden a prolific writer whose writings could enormously transform and empower lives and positively change the world. Put aside your engineering and think twice before hurriedly concluding that you are only an engineer; for you are more than just an engineer.

All over the world, numerous people focus only on their professions and wrongly think that they are not and can never be more than their professions. How wrong they are! You are much more than what you are professionally. I am a professional Mechanical Engineer. However, I do not only stop at my engineering; for I believe that there is so much that I can do outside it. Besides being an engineer, I am, among other things, a researcher, an entrepreneur and a sensational motivational speaker and author whose works have enormously transformed and empowered multitude of people worldwide. If I had focused only on Mechanical Engineering, I would not have discovered that a world-changing researcher, entrepreneur, and motivational speaker and author, among other things, were hidden inside me. I would have never even written this life-transforming book. More still, even with all that I have become, I still believe that there is a lot that I can still do outside and beyond what I am right now. If you put aside your profession and thought of what else you could do apart from it, you would be amazed that you can do so much outside it.

Are you already in your 90s? Have you retired from service into nothing because you think you are too old to do anything? Come-on somebody, even at 90, you still have so much to accomplish. Do not clock 70, 80 or 90 and start counting down days to your death; by doing that, you would be unconsciously telling the world that you are no longer useful to it and therefore you should die. Why invite death so early like that?

Never let your age limit you from achieving more. Age is just a number, do not focus on it; focus on doing and hence achieving more. Some people stop working at 60 while others start at exactly that age or even more. Donald Trump was elected the 45th President of the United States of America at 70, but there are so many people worldwide who have retired into nothing at 70 or even well below that age. If Trump had allowed his age to limit him, he would have never seen the White House as the president of the United States of America. He put his age behind him and dared for the topmost office in the U.S. You too can put your age behind you and focus on doing more.

Do not let your age control you; control it. The bottom line is that you should stop only at death; otherwise as long as you can still breathe, work hard and keep working. The Holy Bible says in Ecclesiastes 11:6 (NIV) that, *"Sow your seed in the morning, and at evening let not your hands be idle, for you do not know which will succeed, whether this or that, or whether both will do equally well."*

Maybe you are supposed to erect an exceptionally powerful business at 95 but if you relax at 60, you will die and be buried with that business in your head. Or perhaps you are supposed to write a life-changing book at 80 but if you choose to relax at 75, what will happen to that book? It will be buried with you when you breathe your last. Can you imagine how many books, businesses, factories, companies, inventions, schools, and hospitals among other things, were buried with people who, during their lifetimes, settled for less than what they could do? Can you go ahead and imagine how wealthy the graveyard is?

Buried deep in the ground is an unimaginable wealth. If you settle for less than what you can do, then you will die with all the things that you could have done and be buried with them. You will then contribute to the great wealth of the graveyard. I challenge you never to do that otherwise the great treasure hidden inside you will never be fully tapped. God created you with your life's purpose to fulfill on earth. You will never fulfill your life's purpose if you ever settle for less than what you can do. By settling for less, you will limit your potential to do and achieve more. A clear sign that you are settling for less is when you feel that there is nothing more you can still do-when you believe that you have done all that you are capable of doing. If you have that feeling, then stop right where you are and rethink to rediscover yourself.

There is always a lot more that you can do. The fact that you are still alive means that there is still something that you can do. Only the dead can do nothing-their fate is already sealed. Do not just relax and wait for death. Even if you are already very old, you can still do so much; one of the most precious things that you can do as an old person is investing in the young people of your area, country or even the whole world. You can nurture them into productive people. Using your great wealth of knowledge, experience and wisdom, you can teach, inspire, encourage, motivate, empower and transform them. The young people need to be guided. You have great knowledge and wisdom which the young people lack.

Whether you are old or young, we should all continuously rediscover ourselves to find out what more we can still do with our abilities. Rediscover yourself and you will realize that there is still so much to do and accomplish. Do not rob the world of your potential. Settle not for what you are right now; for that is still below what you are created to be. You are much more than what you currently consider yourself to be. Do something while you are still able to do it so that you do not regret not doing it while on your death bed.

Whatever can be done today must be done today; for tomorrow has its own obligations. A day will come when you will desire to do something but you may lack both the time and energy to do it; you will regret why you did not do it while you still had both the time and energy. Do not defer what you have in your mind right now; do it. Tomorrow might be too late as you may lack the energy to do it or you could even be dead altogether. The more something is deferred, the higher are its chances of never being done.

Write that book which you are thinking of, implement those business ideas which you have in mind, invent that machine which you have for long been thinking of, start that farm which you have only been envisioning, start that powerful school which you have always thought of or at least lay the foundation stone; maybe this is the school that will fight ignorance in your community, district, country or even the whole world. Construct that house which you have been thinking about. And that hospital which you have been dreaming of? Start it immediately; this could be the hospital that will fight complicated health conditions like cancers which have today become nightmares to the world. That hospital could be hidden inside you right now-let it out.

Have you been thinking about building a church? You are very right; go ahead and build it. This church could win many lost people to God and consequently transform their lives and see them through to heaven. Can you imagine what could happen to those people if you do not build the church which is in your mind?

Has the thought of building an orphanage been haunting you for years? You are on point my great friend. Without wasting any more time, gather the necessary resources and construct that orphanage. Just think of what could happen to the children whom this orphanage is meant to shelter if you do not build it; they could have no place on earth to call home. Maybe you want to establish a humanitarian organization; please do so. Do not overlook it; for God could be calling you to do it. Therefore, give it your all. Whatever you have in mind right now, please endeavour to do it so that you do not die and go with it to the grave. Do not let the grave get even a fraction of your treasure.

Do not underestimate your abilities and please never live below them. Settling for less is so disastrous to the world; it puts the lives of those who should benefit from what you are supposed to do at great risks. Since you were born to do many things from which people are supposed to benefit, if you have been sitting on your abilities, then you have destroyed many lives by not doing what you were supposed to do. Have you ever thought about that? Have you ever imagined how many lives you have unconsciously destroyed by sitting on your abilities? If you are still sitting on your abilities up to now, then you are still destroying more lives. Worse still, if you do not change, then you will destroy even more lives. How unfortunate it is to sit on your abilities and destroy lives! Each of us has at least something on their mind and heart, which they feel that they should do; please do yours.

Do now, all that you are capable of doing now. The more you delay, the more lives you will destroy. Time is running out and will never wait for you. Today, you are nearer to your death than yesterday. If you reach tomorrow, you will even be nearer. In every moment of your life, you get closer to your death. As a matter of fact, you may not even see tomorrow. Therefore, the more you delay, the higher are your chances of dying and hence being buried with all the undone things which you could do. What a waste of potential that would be!

You may not be able to accomplish today, tomorrow or soon, what you plan to do. However, at least lay the foundation and make sure it is a solid one; for just like the strength of a building lies in its foundation, so does the strength of whatever you do. You may not finish something but please start it. At least start that which you conceive. Regardless of who you are, wherever you are in life, where you came from, where you want to go, your family background, what you have and how old you are among other considerations, there is still a lot which you can do. I wonder what is hidden inside you; I challenge you to discover and ultimately exploit it. Go to the grave when you are empty.

CHAPTER TWO
DO NOT BE IN THE CROWD

Jones and his friend Jeff went to Makerere University. Jones hailed from a background where those around him would decide for him. He would not do things without seeking the approval of those with whom he associated. He would confide in them on almost every matter. When he wanted to buy clothes, he would first discuss it with his friends and would buy exactly what they decided. When he wanted to go to a restaurant to have meals, his friends would have to decide for him which one to go to.

When he had no plan, he would automatically go by his friends'. Even when he had one, he would easily and happily sacrifice it for theirs when required. He did exactly what his friends decided. He always took his friends to be responsible for whatever they did together as a group and would blame them for any wrong thing they did. His life was controlled by his friends. He had no personal values that he stood for. He stringently adhered to the principles of the group. His definition of life was entirely that of the group.

He was greatly admonished by the people in the community in which he grew up. However, he never took note of their life-saving advice. Because of his unbecoming behavior, his parents took him to school a little late as they wanted him to first change before he could be taken to school, a dream that would never be realized. They decided to take him to school at the age of 8 anyway. His turning point would not come until he joined the university.

Jeff however, grew up in a setting in which he was taught to always be responsible for whatever he did. He would therefore not do things just because his friends were doing them. He would clearly define whatever he wanted and then lay proper strategies for attaining it. He didn't do as his friends desired but as he planned. He had his personal values which he would never go against; never ever would he compromise his principles just for the sake of his friends or the people around him.

In fact, he would only seriously associate with people who had clear personal visions and goals and were working so hard to achieve them. The first thing he would want to know from whoever got near him was if they had set their goals. In case they had not, he would immediately advise and encourage that person to set them. After which he would then start associating with them. He would consult only trusted people. Discipline and humility were clearly evident in him. Even someone who met him for the very first time would go with at least two things in mind about him; that he was very disciplined and humble.

When he was ready to start school, his parents never hesitated to send him to school. He carried his behaviors to school. He always excelled at his academics. He met Jones in the first semester of their first year at the university. They were all pursuing Bachelor of Science in Computer Engineering. However, they didn't become friends immediately. It was until the second semester that they became very close friends. Jeff emerged the best in the first semester examinations and Jones was the worst student.

One day, they were grouped together for an assignment that was to be done in groups of two students each. They distributed the work among themselves and agreed to go and research and then meet the following day to compile it. Jeff went and did his part to completion. Jones however, went out that night with his friends. He didn't do his part and therefore had nothing to present the following day. When they finally met to compile the work, Jones had completely nothing while Jeff had his well-researched work amassed. He was greatly disappointed by Jones who didn't honor their agreement.

He then asked him what happened, that caused him not to do the work. Jones tried to conceal the facts from Jeff by claiming he did the work but it got lost, something that didn't make any sense to Jeff. Even his own body language could clearly give him away that he was lying. When Jeff later insisted, Jones reluctantly let the cat out of the bag. He narrated to Jeff all that happened. Jeff then talked to him about it. He first told Jones his life history after which he requested him to do the same. After learning Jones' life, Jeff then realized that Jones was in the crowd as his friends would wholly decide for him. Right from his childhood, he would not do things without first consulting his friends and would give up on his plans for those of his friends'.

That is exactly why he did not do his portion of the assignment. That evening, his friends told him they had a plot to go out. He then quickly put down his books and prepared himself for the night. He therefore sacrificed his work for the outing. Because of his lifestyle, he failed miserably in the first semester. Jeff then advised him to set for himself values and principles that he would never go against under the influence of his friends. He even changed his friends. He set his goals and started uncompromisingly pursing them. Jeff helped Jones to get out of the crowd. From that semester onwards, Jones' story totally changed. He was always one of the best students in his class.

From the fable above, we can clearly comprehend a snapshot of the perils of being in the crowd. Jones was flagrantly immersed in the crowd; he always did as decided by the crowd. He would always do what others were doing. His friends constantly decided for him. He had no personal values other than those of the crowd.

Jeff however, had a different mindset. He would do things outside the crowd. He wouldn't allow his friends to decide for him what to do. He had his personal values and principles that he observed at all times. His definition of life was indisputably different from that of Jones.

What about you? Are you in the crowd like Jones or out of it like Jeff? Do you allow your friends to fully decide for you or you carefully weigh out situations before making up your mind? Do you forsake your plans for your friends'? Are you easily influenced by others to do things that are sometimes against your will or you always keep your eyes on what you want? Do you blame other people for the mistakes you make or you take responsibility over them? Do you have your personal values and principles that guide your life? Do you do things just because other people are also doing them or you have your own, clearly defined reasons? Do you join your friends in whatever they are doing or only in what is in line with your values, vision or goals?

Whatever the case, you need to stop where you are and examine your life to see if you are really in the crowd or not. If by any chance you are there, then you need to immediately take action to get out of it and start a new life. It is a very dangerous thing to be in the crowd. In fact, it's catastrophic to identify yourself with the crowd in any way.

Below are 15 dangers of being in the crowd.

A.   You will never discover yourself. The crowd is not a platform for self-discovery. Lack of knowledge of who you are leads to disbelief in yourself. You will settle for less than what you can do and achieve in life; you will never discover and maximize your hidden treasure. You will also never realise and live your life's purpose when you are in the crowd. Everyone has their life's purpose which cannot be realized within the crowd. Being out of the crowd gives you the capacity to discover yourself and hence maximize your potential and realise your life's purpose.

B.   You will not see or tap opportunities that lie beyond the crowd. This is because you will think only within the crowd. You will never think outside the crowd hence whatever opportunity lies outside it, you will most likely miss. You cannot therefore dream big in life within the crowd. Those in the crowd can't explore new horizons through their thoughts and actions as they are confined. The crowd is like a box; within which they fully operate.

All their thoughts and actions are within it. They can't see beyond it hence can't envision opportunities outside it. It's only those not in the crowd who can see and tap the opportunities that lie beyond it. Such people always think outside the box and explore new limits.

C.   The crowd will hold you back from your success. In fact, those with whom you are in the crowd will be jealous with whatever success you attain; they will incessantly fight to bring you down because they will not want you to succeed any more than them. Within the crowd, you cannot therefore position yourself to achieve great things. While in the crowd, your achievements are those of the crowd, hence your success is measured by the standards of the crowd. Successful people don't do things in the crowd; they separate themselves from it and then pursue their interests. You can't succeed when in the crowd; you can't achieve great things within the crowd.

D.   You will have no clear vision and goals for your life. Those in the crowd have no clear visions and targets for their lives. Hence by default, you won't be exceptional in anyway. If you have a different mission from those in the crowd, you can't live with them as you will surely have conflicting interests. If you ask anyone who is in the crowd, where they want to be 5, 10 or 20 years from now, they can barely give you an answer. This is because those in the crowd normally do not see beyond the present; they don't envision the future so that they could plan for it.

If you are among them, then you will not have the capacity to define what you want in life, where you want to be by a particular time and how to get there. You will be deprived of your right to make proper decisions for your life. You will therefore chase the wind in the name of working so hard to build your life. Thus to clearly define your goals and vision and realize them, you have to be out of the crowd.

E.   You will never live your life. When in the crowd, you will strive to live the lives of others; you will be too quick to admire other people's lives at the expense of your own. You will thus value other people more than you value yourself. You will always compare yourself with other people, often thinking and believing that they are better than you. Hence you will compete with them, always wanting to get on top of them. To you, life will mean nothing but competing with other people. If you really want to value your life, then you have to be out of the crowd.

F.   You will lose your personal identity. When you are in the crowd, you will sacrifice who you are for what the crowd is. You will always need other people's approvals to feel important and valuable. You will go by what others feel, say or believe about yourself. It will be very difficult to motivate yourself to do things or pursue your interests in life as your energy will come from the crowd. Hence you will have low self-esteem as you will feel you are nothing without the crowd. You will thus hardly be proud of yourself.

G.   You will not be responsible for your life. Being in the crowd will make you waste your life due to irresponsibility. It's very hard to do the right things when in the crowd. You will venture into non-productive things that you will surely live to regret later. There will come a time in your life when the things that once mattered so much to you-those you used to do with the crowd- will no longer appeal to you. That's when you will realize that you wasted valuable time pursuing useless things. After so many years of laboring so hard, you will have nothing to count on as your achievements. Only regrets will be your rewards. Take full responsibility over your life. Don't trade it cheaply by being in the crowd.

H.   You will have no personal values. Your values will automatically be those of the crowd. You will be forced by the crowd to do things which are against your will. You will not be in control of your life but will unconsciously hand it over to the crowd. It will be very hard for you to stand for what is right when the crowd doesn't accept it. You will easily engage in criminal acts like corruption, stealing, killing, abortion and many others when you are in the crowd.

The problem is that whatever the crowd decides, you have to go by unless you want to be an enemy of the crowd in which case you can suffer serious consequences like being excommunicated, losing your job, friends, and even sometimes your own life. For example, in case the crowd decides that someone should be killed and you refuse, even though you are right as life should not be taken by people, you may be killed for your refusal to take part in the gruesome act.

I.   You will hardly glorify God with your life. God created you to serve Him with your all. This won't happen when you are in the crowd. It's impossible for you to live right with God when in the crowd. God's laws become a great burden to you. For example, where the law says, "Do not steal…" and one of your activities is stealing, you will hardly obey the law. Therefore, you cannot develop your personal relationship with God within the crowd.

You have to separate yourself from the crowd so as to have intimacy with God. This doesn't mean you don't have to associate with those who do not know God. Just like Jesus Christ associated with such people so should you; and your presence among them should cause them to know God or at least know about Him. You have to preach to them so that they may believe and hence change. You only have to make sure you don't get assimilated by them. You have to live like Christ did among those who did not know God. Do not compromise your standards as a Christian for the sake of non-Christians.

You can live among Pagans as a Christian without sacrificing your Christianity for their paganism. While there, you have a great task of preaching to the pagans so that they come to the knowledge of God. You do not have to do the wrong things they do, that displease God but at all times you must stand for what is right even if it means being killed for it. Jesus Christ stood for and preached what was right even among those who didn't obey God. As Christians, we have to do the same. We shouldn't compromise our standards for whatsoever reason. We have to be out of the crowd so that we can effectively and efficiently do the will of God.

J.   You will always be a victim of blame game. If you are in the crowd, blame game will be one of your most revered tools for comforting yourself whenever you fail in something. You will always blame circumstances and other people for all the wrong things you do as well as your failures even when you are entirely responsible for them. You will look for excuses whenever you don't realize your prospects or fall short of what is expected of you or what you expected.

You will always say things like: "The road was too bad," "No one helped me," "I wasn't favored like other people," "So and so made me do it," "I am too short," "If only I had what others had, I would have made it," "I am not good enough," "I lacked money to do it," "I don't have what it takes to succeed," "No one believes in me,"

"If only I was born in a rich family, my situation would have been better" "I am very unlucky," "I am very poor," "Someone is bewitching me," "I wish so and so were my parents," and many other excuses or limiting beliefs. You will never acknowledge your own role in your misdeeds. You cannot therefore better your life as you will always be backed up by the blame game.

If you find yourself in a situation like the one above, then please immediately do something about it. Change the course of your life. You are surely following the wrong path. Stop blaming circumstances or people for what happens in your life. Examine yourself to know your contribution to the results you get. That will help you to be careful before you act as you will be mindful of the consequences. In fact, before doing something, first think about the consequences. For surely whatever you do will affect you in some way.

K.   You will be more of a liability to the society than an asset. If you follow the standards set by the crowd, then you will often be a nuisance to the society. Most, if not all, of the wrong doers of the society are in the crowd. Those in the crowd tend to have their own rules which in most cases directly conflict with those of the society. They therefore mostly contribute negatively to the society. For example, burglars, killers, rapists, corrupt individuals and all other wrong elements do the society more harm than good.

If you are not in the crowd, then you will have less chances of committing crimes as you will always think for yourself and be responsible for what you do. You can easily control yourself in any circumstance outside the crowd. You will know the limit of doing things and will easily observe the laws of the society.

L.   You will frequently be frustrated in life. Frustration normally results when you do not meet your expectations in life. When you are in the crowd, you cannot find proper solutions to your issues as they may be outside the crowd. And also no one in the crowd including yourself is fully responsible for your affairs. Therefore, even though you do things together, you have to be responsible for the consequences which in most cases you are not. Worse still, when you are in the crowd, you will often seek advice from the wrong people. The wrong advice you are given only worsens your situation.

For example, a school boy called Martin Opiro once drank alcohol with his peer group members and was suspended from school yet the other members were not even noticed to have also been drunk. It was Martin's first ever encounter with alcohol. He later asked the group leader, called Alex, about what to do as he had been suspended. Alex told him to go home and drink as much alcohol as he could so that when he reported back to school after the suspension period, he would be an expert and wouldn't therefore be noticed when drunk. Martin went home and seriously embarked on drinking alcohol.

He drank to the extent where he would even sleep in bars and other drinking joints. He would sometimes drink so much that he would fail to reach home; on such occasions, he would sometimes spend the night wherever dusk found him unless someone, out of kindness, took him home. It was only the intervention of his mother that saved him. She did not only carefully counsel him but also took him to a different school. He was in the crowd and sought advice within it-from the wrong person. You can't have the right mentors within the crowd; they are outside it.

You will be greatly dissatisfied with your life when in the crowd. You will also easily give up when things become tough. However, when you are not in the crowd, you can plan better, and also seek advice from the right people-those whom you can trust and have confidence in. Such people can guide you in life so that you don't go astray.

M.   It will be very difficult for you be corrected. With the life-destroying character you develop while in the crowd, you will hardly listen to and lay hold of advice from the right people. Therefore, you can't easily be corrected when you go off track. Those in the crowd normally take long to get out of it because they hardly accept advice from those outside it. They believe they are always right. If you don't acknowledge your mistakes, then you can't be corrected. If you should easily be corrected in life, then make sure you aren't in the crowd.

N.   You will hardly be trusted by other people. Trusting someone who is in the crowd is like entrusting a hungry dog with your roasted piece of meat; you should fully blame yourself when the dog eats it up. It's hard to be honest when in the crowd. Trust is built on honesty. If you are dishonest, then you can't be trusted by anyone. In fact, within the crowd, you will be dishonest first with yourself, then other people. Even those with whom you are in the crowd won't trust you. That's why within the crowd, treachery is inevitable among members. Everybody wants to gain more than the rest. This makes them greatly dishonest. If you want to be trusted, then you have to be honest and to achieve this, you have to be outside the crowd. The society doesn't trust, believe in and count on those in the crowd.

O.   Your life's progress will be delayed. Living in the crowd will greatly thwart your efforts no matter how much you try. It's only until you get out of the crowd that you will begin to see the reality of life. Doing things as decided by the crowd will block you from building your life. By the time you dissociate yourself from the crowd and start concentrating on your life, you will have lost a lot, which you could have achieved if you had not been in the crowd.

* * * * * *

Being in the crowd poses you to numerous dangers. Not all of them are exhausted here. In a nutshell, if you are in the crowd, you cannot think for yourself; the crowd will automatically think for you. Your life will be controlled by the crowd. You will act according to what the crowd deems fit and necessary. You will live your life based on the standards set by the crowd. Everything you do is dependent on the crowd. If you are not in the crowd, then you can think for yourself, set your standards and principles that you live by and you will be unique in all you do.

Don't do something just because other people are doing it. Define clearly why you have to do it. Just because everyone is doing something does not necessarily mean it is good or the right thing to do. Corruption, rape, defilement, robbery, killing, cheating and other immoral acts are always abhorred no matter who is doing them. Likewise, just because no one is doing something is no indication that it's bad or the wrong thing to do.

Helping others, campaigning against immoral acts, observing laws and cultivating the right values among others will always be virtuous even if no one is doing them. You have to know why you must do something.

Never jump onto a wagon without first of all finding out where it is going. It might lead you to where you will live to regret for the rest of your life. To better position yourself to do and achieve great things in life, you have to separate yourself from the crowd.

You need to have an independent mindset from that of the crowd, look at life from an angle which is different from that of the crowd and change the way you perceive life. Don't get assimilated by those in the crowd otherwise you will lose your individuality. Whatever you do will be dictated by the crowd. Your creativity will be greatly limited. If you are in the crowd, you will never go further than the crowd. Do not follow the crowd; stand out from it. You were not created to follow the crowd but to set yourself apart that the world may count on you. Make that choice and live it.

Don't let others influence you to make decisions and do things that ruin your life; be in charge of your life. If your friends exclusively decide for you, then you are not fully in charge of your life. You have unconsciously handed it over to them such that they choose whatever they want to do with it.

To make a difference, you have to be different; you must not be in the crowd. Some people are in the crowd unconsciously while others chose to be there. The crowd is clearly the wrong environment for living your life. No positive life development can take place there. If you are already in it, then get out immediately. It is a matter of urgency and should be given the seriousness it deserves. If you are not there yet, then strive with all your might never to get there. You cannot afford to be in the crowd if you really want to make it in life. By changing your mindset and making the decision to stop following the crowd, you can get out of it.

If you choose to remain in the crowd, you will only count the losses in future whereas if you choose to get out of it, then you will gladly rejoice in future when you compare your life while still in the crowd with the one after getting out of it. Definitely you will achieve great things outside the crowd; things you would never ever achieve while in the crowd. Make the choice to get out of the crowd today if you are there. The results will amaze you. And if you are not there, then help others to get out of it just like Jeff helped his friend Jones.

There are so many people around you who are in the crowd. They may not even be aware of it. Still some people are greatly dissatisfied with their lives, because they are in the crowd and want to withdraw from it yet do not know how to do it. Bring them to the reality of how to get out of the crowd. Help them out; show them the way.

Don't be selfish with your life outside the crowd. Don't refuse to help others; be humble enough to support other people to get out of the crowd. Be nice to those in the crowd; they could change because of you. Jeff treated Jones nicely; he never condemned him. In the end, Jones opened up to Jeff and he helped him to get out of the crowd.

If you are in the crowd, to get out of it, you have the greatest role to play. Other people can always help you but unless you play your role well, you won't be able to get out of the crowd. If Jones didn't play his role, Jeff wouldn't help him much. It's impossible for other people to help you if you don't take responsibility by playing your role. You have to make a decision to get out of the crowd and then other people will help you to get out of it. One of the critical things you should always do if you are in the crowd is to pray to God to enable you to get out of it so that you can fulfill your life's purpose. He knows you better than anyone else including yourself. He is the best person to help you get out of and stay outside the crowd.

The society should make sure children are brought up outside the crowd. They should be taught to always be responsible for whatever they do. If they grow up in the crowd, then it will be very difficult for them to be responsible adults in future. The reason why some adults are problematic to the society today is because they grew up in the crowd. They had no personal values that they stood for when they were young. Some of the people who misappropriate funds in public offices today started stealing in their childhood with their friends.

Still some of the drunkards in the community today had their first ever encounter with alcohol when they were young. For many people, the root of the wrong things they do today can be traced back to their childhood. For such people, the wrong foundation of life was laid in their lives. Most of the wrong things in the society today could have been avoided if the people who are responsible for them were brought up rightly. We should therefore be mindful of how we raise children because they tend to carry on with their childhood behaviors to adulthood. The Holy Bible says in Proverbs 22:6 (NIV) that, *"Train a child in the way he should go, and when he is old he will not turn from it."*

To model the children outside the crowd, you first need to be outside it. You can't teach someone to be responsible when you are not. By being irresponsible, you won't know what it means to be responsible and you can't teach someone what you don't know. To save the future, we need to take care of the present and make it count. We can't do that within the crowd. The bottom line is, if you really want to achieve great things in life, then you have to separate yourself from the crowd at all cost. It's only outside the crowd that you can truly be yourself; within it, you will always fake personalities.

Don't sacrifice what you are for what the crowd is. Don't give up what you believe in for what the crowd believes in. Don't surrender your values so as to identify with some people. Even though you are alone, go on. Don't just join other people or ask them to join you because you are alone. Join them or ask them to join you because they will help you achieve what you desire. Standing out from the crowd doesn't mean you have to be independent in life. Remember the popular adage, "No man is an island of his own." In life, you have to work with other people. They are necessary for your progress and success. You cannot live alone. You have to embrace other people. Only that you have to choose wisely the people who should be in your life. The right people will help you to achieve your targets whereas the wrong ones will ruin you.

You are responsible for the people you allow into your life. Be careful with those who come into your life as they can either make or break you. Those who will make you are not in the crowd; those who will break you are there. No one can make you while operating from the crowd; they have to first get out of it. Therefore, if you want to choose the right people to be in your life, first you have to be out of the crowd and then from there, you will get them. Whenever you associate with the right people and in the right environment, then you are in a proper position to make it in life. Endeavour to always live outside the crowd in order to be able to ultimately make use of your hidden treasure.

CHAPTER THREE
FOCUS ON YOUR MISSION

A hunter once set out to hunt a lion which had disturbed his village for a very long time. It had terrorized the village, killing many people and domestic animals, causing the people to live in constant fear as any time it could show up while scouting its prey. The people couldn't even till their gardens anymore even though most of them were on the outskirts of the village.

When the day dawned on which the hunter was to go for the lion, all his people, both young and old, gathered at his home to pray for and bless him as he embarked on the journey that could rescue the people from the worries, fears, vexations and psychological turmoils that had engulfed them for a long time. Everyone laid their hands on him as they said prayers for the "savior" of the village. He gathered all his hunting gears-spear, bow and arrows among others as well as some foodstuffs and set off for the forest in which the lion lived.

He was exceptionally determined and focused to kill the lion and bring its head home so as to bring an end to the nightmare of the village. The forest was quite far from the village, about seven hills away with the distance from one hill to the next averaging about five miles. He could therefore have to walk a long distance before encountering the lion.

The road was also very rough as by that time, no one could follow it for fear that they might encounter the lion and hence consequently meet their death. The hunter sauntered through the bushy road, clearing the way with some of his hunting gears so that he could stride through the bushy thickets.

When he had gone midway between the sixth and seventh hills, an antelope crossed his path. All along that he had been walking, his focus and attention were solely on looking out for the lion. However, no sooner had he seen the antelope than his attention wholly shifted to it. He started relentlessly chasing the antelope, running after it while striking his spear and arrows towards it, praying that they could land on it. Pretty soon, he succeeded when one of the arrows he sent forth after the antelope successfully landed on its head, striking it through the left ear to the other side.

The poor antelope fell down, bleeding copiously, and breathed its last. The man came, threw his hunting gears apart and started dancing, while singing songs of joy in celebration for having killed the antelope. He blew his hands, whistled, jumped from one side to another and danced around the lifeless antelope openly expressing his unimaginable delight as he planned to skin it. He completely forgot that he set out from the village to hunt the lion not the antelope. At this juncture, the lion was only a short distance away from where he was. He was so blindfolded by the joy of killing the antelope that he forgot why he left his wife and children and the entire village, risked his life and came to the forest. Instead of controlling his emotions after killing the antelope, they controlled him. He later picked his knife and started skinning the animal while still singing and shouting at the top of his voice.

By this time of the day, the lion had surveyed the seventh hill looking for a prey to devour. However, its struggle was in vain; it had caught nothing and was inestimably hungry and would therefore pay whatever price to catch any prey it would, by any chance, come across. It slept under a very tall huge tree in the interior of the hill, to temporarily relax in its cool shade as the sunshine was hot and plaguing. It rested under the tree, breathing like an extremely hungry person who has just successfully completed a marathon race and is therefore dying to both eat and rest. A shade was there for the lion to rest under but there was nothing to eat. It therefore rested uneasily under the shade even though it was so imperturbable, characterized by the cool breeze from the undulating thick-forested hill in the middle of which the tree stood.

As the lion lay under the shade, it kept all its ears and eyes open, to sense any prey that might avail itself so that it could pursue it for its banquet. Suddenly, the noise the hunter was making reached the lion's ears, tipping it that a prey could be within its vicinity. This prompted it to quickly get up and begin tracking the noise; it started moving slowly, in the direction from which the noise was emanating. The noise became louder and louder as it approached the hunter, who was still skinning the antelope. As the lion drew nearer to him, it became continually assured that it was on the verge of catching its prey and hence finding what to feast on at least for that moment in which it was dying of the furious hunger.

When it finally saw the hunter, whose excitement was at the peak as he mercilessly skinned his prey, the lion salivated ultimately and started aggressively running towards him for there was no time to waste; food was already at its disposal. It only had to work just a little harder to find its sharp teeth on its "banquet". The hunter was completely ignorant of whatever was going on; he was by this time, concentrating only on skinning the antelope. By the time he saw the lion and reminisced that he had come to hunt it not the antelope and any other animal, it was already too late for him to save himself.

He realized that he was in an unimaginable menace. He looked around for his hunting tools only to see some of them scattered all over the place; he couldn't even trace some as he threw them out of excitement after killing the antelope and never even saw where they landed. He could in no way gather them to fight the lion, which was approaching at breakneck speed. He was therefore at the mercy of the lion which was unfortunately very hungry and could not spare him. The lion hastily jumped onto the helpless hunter, caught and ate him completely together with his dead antelope.

The hunter died with his mission unrealized. He never fulfilled the purpose for which he went to the forest. He never saved his village from the ferocious lion. He only added salt to the wounds of his people. His family would miss him; his wife and children would have no one to look after them. The lion took him by the storm and saw him off.

Like the hunter in the story who set out to hunt the lion, many of us often set out to do something with all our focus and attention on it at its commencement. However, along the way, we come across other things and completely shift our attention and focus to them. We end up failing to accomplish what we had initially set out to do. The end results are sometimes catastrophic as many lives can be lost. A lot of time, energy and other resources are wasted. We end up chasing the wind in the name of success.

It is therefore paramount to always keep your eyes on the lion you set out to hunt so that it does not take you by the storm and hence devour you. If you don't hunt your "lion", it might hunt you to death. It is hungry and looking for what to eat and you are its prey. Don't become the hunted; remain the hunter. Sometimes it's necessary to first kill the antelope that crosses your path to give you the green light to hunt the lion. In that case, kill it but never forget that your mission is to hunt and kill the lion. The antelope is just a stepping stone to hunting the lion. Always keep that in mind.

Once you have killed the antelope, the way is then clear for you to continue to face the lion. Waste no time on the dead antelope; move on and kill the lion. Don't kill the antelope and throw away your hunting tools out of excitement like the imprudent hunter. Remember the lion you set out to kill and remain focused on it. The hunter's negligence of his mission eventually led to his death. Killing the lion carries more rewards than killing the antelope. However, sometimes killing the latter is a prerequisite to killing the former. Whatever the case, don't forget your lion which is your mission. If you kill the antelope and start celebrating, it won't be possible to gather all your tools that may be scattered all over the place in a very short time to fight the advancing and aggressive lion.

What "lion" did you set out to hunt? Where have you reached? What "antelope" has crossed your path? How are you handling it? Have you forgotten the "lion" or you are still focused on it? Have you forgotten your mission or you are still pursuing it? Have you sacrificed your "lion" for your "antelope"? Don't forget your mission; pursue it incessantly. Just like the lion never stops chasing its prey until it catches it, so must you chase your dreams until you realize them. Joking with your dreams has far reaching consequences on you, your people, community, country and the world at large. Sometimes it can put the lives of very many people at great risks. The hunter brought a great loss not only to his family but also his village at large. Instead of saving his people from their existing predicaments, he only worsened their status quo because he joked with his mission; he didn't stay true to it. He betrayed his people by not sticking to his mission.

How serious are you with your mission? Are you mindful of the fact that joking with it is catastrophic? Don't slacken off, procrastinate or compromise for any reason. Be married to your mission and sacrifice for it. Your mission could save your people, community, district, region, country and the world. Don't add to the pain of the people in your community by playing with your mission. The Holy Bible says in Ecclesiastes 9:10 (NIV) that, *"Whatever your hand finds to do, do it with all your might, for in the grave, where you are going, there is neither working nor planning nor knowledge nor wisdom."*

Therefore, chase your mission wholeheartedly. While doing so, don't forget that the antelope may cross your path. Chasing your mission however, is not a walk-over; you will walk through thorns that will prick you and indomitable fires that will surely scorch you. You will climb steep mountains, cross deep valleys and sail through stormy waters. You will get a lot of discouragements and criticisms from people, some of whom could even be saved by your mission. However, no matter the challenges that come your way, don't give up; persevere and persist till you realize your mission.

Whatever you encounter along the way shouldn't make you forget your mission. Don't become the hunted just because you shift your focus from the lion to the antelope. It's only until you kill the lion that you can be crowned. At all times keep your eyes on your mission till you realize it.

CHAPTER FOUR
TAP YOUR POTENTIAL

When I, together with a friend, once visited a professor, he took us to a cemetery bordering his home to the southwest; just a few meters away from it. At first both I and Angel, for that was my friend's name, were astonished by what was happening; we couldn't clearly comprehend it. We both feared to step into the cemetery. However, he told us to be bold enough to walk into it with him. When we entered, he instructed us to walk around in the cemetery and carefully observe everything after which he would then ask each of us to tell him the lessons we would have learnt. We were to take different directions and not focus on whatever the other would be doing as that would affect our concentration since our attention would be divided. He sternly instructed us to focus on whatever we would see and envision.

He went out and stood at the rust-brown metallic gate of the cemetery. Our assignment, which was to take exactly 30 minutes, then began. Both Angel and I looked at each other horrifically. I noticed how frightened she was, an indication that she could have never been to a cemetery before and yet there she was surrounded by graves all over. I started walking gently, taking the southern direction; moving from one grave to another, I read the inscriptions on the tombstones. Some were visible while others were almost not clear. Later, Angel also took her direction, tiptoeing slowly and horrendously among the copious graves in the eastern direction which she took. As I walked majestically among the graves, I noticed what was written on one of them. I was amazed and beads of tears started forming in my eyes. It was written that, "Where you are, I was and where I am, you will be; it's just a matter of time. Live your life responsibly; make it count every day. Hold back nothing and die empty. To not live your life's purpose is a grave mistake." This among the many things which I saw and learnt in the cemetery stunned me.

Pretty soon, the 30 minutes were over and the professor summoned us. We then sat under a mango tree in front of his house. The looks on our faces could make someone believe that we were from the world of the dead. Even the professor himself was scared since the excitement with which we entered his thrilling compound had vanished in thin air. It was then time to share what each of us had learnt. Angel was to go first.

"I told you from the beginning that today you would learn the best lessons of your lives. So what did you people learn?" asked the professor, expectantly.

"I learnt that while you are alive, you should treat people well. Don't treat yourself as if you are superior; no one is superior to anyone in this world; we are all children of God. Be compassionate, humble, peaceful, loving, prayerful and faithful. When we die, to the dust we all return as from it, we all came. We don't own the world we live in; we are just passing through it. The world isn't our destiny. This is from what I saw on the graves," answered Angel, looking a bit relieved.

"Wow! That's great, Angel. What a great lesson!" remarked the professor, sounding ecstatic.

Turning to me, he asked, "and you, Lazarus?"

I was lost in thoughts at this point but I had to quickly recollect myself to narrate my tale of what transpired.

"Well, I realized that there's nothing as important as life; it's so precious that we have to guard it jealously. We can't create it; therefore, we shouldn't take it. It's something very sacred. On one of the graves it was written that the deceased was innocently slaughtered. As human beings, we should really value life. Only God has the right to take it. I also learnt that we are born empty materially and we leave this earth the same way. It doesn't really matter how much you have achieved. The houses which you have built, the cars you own and other assets accumulated. Everything you have labored so much to gather will all be left on earth when you breathe your last. What then should you do? Just one thing; yes, one thing; live your life for God and entrust it fully to Him. The best thing you can ever do on earth is to serve

God with your life. We should therefore give ourselves fully to serving God. There's nothing we can gain from this world and die and go with.

Finally, I also learnt that in the grave lies a lot of untapped potential. A lot of people lived lives of unfulfilled dreams and unrealized potential. They never discovered the purposes for which they were created and therefore never lived those purposes. We should therefore discover and fulfill the purposes for which we were created; only then shall we leave behind a legacy the world will remember us for if we die. It is just a matter of choice; we can choose to discover or not, our respective purposes. The bottom line is we should wholly serve God with our lives as a life not lived for God is a life wasted," I answered, with a serious look on my face. By this time, both the professor and Angel were looking at me the way a hungry dog looks at meat being roasted in an incarcerated area.

"Wow! Wow! Wooooooow! This is incredible Lazarus. I can see you had a soul-awakening adventure in the cemetery. While you were speaking, I heard what I had never made out before. I have been walking into this cemetery for years but hadn't learnt what you said. I am so proud of you two; you visited me today and learnt a lot as I can see. From this point, I'm sure you guys will look at life differently," he remarked, joyfully.

"Oh yes, Sir!" Both Angel and I, answered in unison.

"Now go and take the necessary precautions. And make the most of your lives," he said as he dismissed us. "Thanks a lot professor for the life-transforming lessons. God bless you mightily. Good-bye," we said as we bade farewell to him and vacated his lonely homestead.

Angel later asked me why I took her to see the professor who tortured her that much, because according to her submissions, assuredly she had never been to a cemetery; never before had she even ever imagined herself just standing in a cemetery, yet she had to tour one that day. I later encouraged her to be strong and told her that what transpired wasn't even the least of what I expected. We went back with different mindsets; the way each of us viewed life had enormously changed.

I didn't really want to write this anecdote you are reading right now, however, the thought of it being helpful in awakening someone made me pen down what happened chronologically. Have you ever been to a cemetery?
Maybe; maybe not. However, even though you haven't been there, at least you know how it looks like and how lonely it is. In fact, one of the quietest places on earth is the cemetery. It's really bloodcurdling to even imagine yourself standing there. Do you know why? Because while there, you would be surrounded all over by graves. However, what remains true is that those in the graves

were once like us, and we will one day be like them; it's just a matter of time. This is a fact we can't dispute.

But how do we die and join those who are already in the cemetery? You will agree with me that the world over, a lot of people have gone to their graves with their potential untapped. Some of them never even discovered theirs so that they could utilize it; while others discovered theirs but because they were too obsessed with other people's lives, they wanted to live exactly like them. They ended up failing to live their own lives and hence their potential was untapped; they died and went down the earth, with their potential unexploited. How ill-fated that is! What a waste of potential!

Most people don't ever seek to discover why they were created. They, therefore, do not get to know the purposes for their lives. When you ask such people why they were created, they have no answer; not even a clue can they give you. They live as if they came to earth just to tour it. Many people live lives of unfulfilled purposes simply because they cannot even for a second think that there should be at least a reason for which they were created. You were created not just to pass through the earth but to bring something new into it-to transform it. How can you do that? By discovering and living your life's purpose.

It is your responsibility to discover why you were created. You cannot live your life's purpose unless you first discover it. It takes strenuous efforts to discover your life's purpose. Without the discovery of your purpose, you will live a purposeless life and die and go down into the grave with untapped potential. There is a purpose for which everything was created.

As human beings, we are meant to subdue the earth, to positively transform it; however, for that to happen, we have to discover our purposes first. Without discovering what you came to earth to do, you can't be a person of positive impact. Do you know why? Because you are meant to change the world by discovering and living your life's purpose. A lot of people think that for them to positively transform the world or be influential, they must first occupy certain positions in life or own certain things. Others think they should first be extremely rich- they should own luxurious houses, drive the most expensive cars and hold billions on their bank accounts among others. This is a fallacy. Your true wealth is your potential; no one can take it away from you.

No one is born with money, house, car or plane. We all find and leave these things on earth. They are all of no use to a dead person. Yet everyone was created with a lot of potential. Your potential is your treasure. What legacy will you leave behind when you die? What will the world miss you for if you breathe your last? In other words, what contributions are you making to the world? What are you doing to make the world a better place; to positively transform it? I challenge you to fully discover yourself, get to know the purpose for which you were created, know your potential and ultimately tap it. Once you do that, even if you die physically, you will still live in the minds of those who will remember you for the great things you will have done.

Believe me Nelson Mandela will always be remembered as one of the people who colossally transformed the world. He wasn't any exceptional neither was he superior; he just discovered his life's purpose and lived it. He did not desire to live another man's life. One of the greatest mistakes you can ever make, that will prevent you from discovering and hence living your purpose, is trying to live other people's lives. You are created to live your idiosyncratic life. You can't be influential and make a difference in the world when you are trying to live the lives of others. Those the world considers to be great never try to live other people's lives; they live their own lives.

To become a master in your game, you have to be yourself. No one is another person's prototype. Don't just seek to become like someone; seek to discover yourself. This is because once you know yourself, then you are good to go, for no one can then cause you to disbelieve in yourself. And please don't compare yourself with others; remember they have different lives to live and you have your own to live also. You can, however, learn from them. While doing so, always keep in mind that you are unique in your own way. How influential you are is not measured by the difference between you and other people but by the difference between what you do and what you were created to do.

You may not do what others can do, have done or will do but that does not mean that you cannot live your purpose. We have different abilities; that is why we do things differently and levels of achievements as well do vary. The fact that someone has more money than you does not mean that you have missed your mark or they have achieved more than you. However wealthy you are, unless you discover your purpose for creation, you will live a purposeless life. You will die with all your potential and be buried with it. I know of no better way of putting your potential to waste than this.

Some people get to know their purposes but fail to live them and hence never fulfill them. I am normally amazed by those who struggle so much to know other people's lives. They spend a lot of time studying other people, trying to get to know them but they don't spend time to know themselves. They know other people more than they know themselves. This is a clear indication that someone has lost their life's course. Such people can't leave behind a legacy that the world can admire when they die. Sincerely how do you expect to become a better person today than you were yesterday if you don't even know yourself? You can't better what you don't know.

If you really want to grow and mature in life, and live responsibly, then you have to be in proper knowledge of yourself. Living your purpose starts with knowing yourself first. You have to do self-evaluation to determine the kind of person you are so that you can become what you want to become. Time spent getting to know yourself is time never wasted. We all need to consistently examine ourselves so that we can become what we desire to become and therefore better our lives. The dead can in no way reverse their conditions yet the living still have a lot of chances to become what they're created to be. Continually spend time with yourself so that you get to know yourself more.

Just like the manufacturer of a particular product knows best what their product is made for, so does your creator knows best what you were created for. Therefore, to discover God's purpose for your life, you have to ask Him since He is your creator. You can never discover your purpose outside God. He created you to do something on earth; He is therefore the one to reveal to you what He created you to do. He created you with gifts and talents which are your tools for fulfilling your purpose. Everybody is gifted in certain fields. The Holy Bible says in Proverbs 18:16 (NKJV) that, *"A man's gift makes room for him, and brings him before great men."*

Your gifts open doors to opportunities for you. You will go to places which otherwise you would never visit, you will meet people whom otherwise you would only dream of even just seeing, you will hold positions in life which otherwise you would never hold; you will do many things with your gifts. Your gifts are very powerful; please never joke with them. To fully discover your gifts, ask God to reveal them to you; He is the source of gifts. And to fully tap your hidden treasure, you need to be in the presence of God. When a fish is taken out of water, it suffocates and dies, and when a plant is pulled out of the ground, it perishes; similarly, when man is out of God's presence, he malfunctions and dies spiritually. In the wrong environment, you can never fully tap your hidden treasure. God's presence is the only environment for ultimately exploiting your hidden treasure.

Once you discover your purpose, give it your all. Hold back nothing. Do not die with untapped potential; die when you are totally empty. Die like Paul the Apostle who, towards his death, said, *"For I am already being poured out like a drink offering, and the time has come for my departure. I have fought the good fight, I have finished the race, I have kept the faith. Now there is in store for me the crown of righteousness, which the Lord, the righteous Judge, will award to me on that day-and not only to me but also to all who have longed for his appearing"* (2 Timothy 4:6-8, NIV).

Paul died having fulfilled the purpose for which he was created. Will you speak like him at the time of your death, because you will have fulfilled the purpose for which you were created? Do not go into the grave with unexploited potential and unrealized purpose. Discover your purpose today and live it. Do not wait till it is too late to do the needful. You have limited time on earth but that time, when utilized well, is enough for you to fulfill your life's purpose.

CHAPTER FIVE
PLAN PROPERLY

Two men once set out to travel to a distant place. They were on a mission to survey a land which their king wanted to conquer for his kingdom. The land was believed to be unimaginably wealthy. It was said to be having abundant quantities of gold, silver, mercury and diamond among other things on top of being exceptionally fertile. The king was more than determined to take it at any cost given its great wealth.

However, he first sought to be sure the land had exactly what he wanted. So he sent two of his emissaries to find out. They were to tour the land and discover as much information as they could about it. Based on their report, the king would then make a proper decision on whether to attack the inhabitants of the land and take away the land or not.

The men prepared for the great task ahead of them. They collected the resources that they would need to carry out the task; among others things, they collected foodstuffs, heavy and warm clothes and fighting tools to help them in case they were attacked by strangers and wild animals. They were then blessed by the king and elders of the kingdom, who prayed for their safety and accomplishment of the task. Above all, they prayed that the land should contain exactly what they wanted so that the efforts of these men would not be void.

After many hours of prayers, they were then flagged off by the king and kingdom elders to go forth and tour the land which the king was more than enthusiastic to take. They would be greatly rewarded for the task if they succeeded; the king promised them that gold, silver, diamond and part of the land among other things, would be their rewards. They were therefore more than motivated to diligently carry out the task as the rewards seemed to be greater than the risks even though they could die in the process as they had no idea about what they would encounter in the process of carrying out the task. Nevertheless, they were more than willing to do it with all their might till they achieved their targets.

The men set off from the king's palace for the place which was over three hundred miles from the village. They trekked through thick bushes, clearing them with their hatchets in order to create way for them. Two days down the road, they were already tired even though they were still far from covering half the distance to the place. One of them suggested that they should go back as the task seemed onerous and impossible. However, the colleague vehemently refused. He said he didn't start to stop on the way, but to finish the task. He advised his friend that they shouldn't focus on the challenges they were encountering, but on their rewards after achieving their goals.

They rested under one of the big trees after which they continued with their journey. After a long spell of walking, they got very close to the village; something that brought a great joy to their hearts. However, this joy was, but only temporary as they soon saw a very huge mountain ahead of them. The mountain was covering the road; they would have to climb it in order to reach the village.

The man who had earlier suggested going back to the village gasped in disbelief as he thought it was surely impossible to climb the mountain. His colleague however, being a positive-minded person, upon seeing the mountain, told him that they should figure out how to climb it so that at the end of the day, they could achieve their targets. He suggested that before they reach the mountain, they should make ropes and collect other resources to climb it. The colleague however, said it wouldn't be possible to climb the mountain. When his friend insisted that they could climb it, he said unless he first got close to the mountain, he wouldn't waste time to look for the ropes to climb it. So he watched as his friend made ropes from the forest trees.

They then proceeded with their journey. The closer they got to the mountain, the bigger it became. Pretty soon, they reached it. It was actually a very big mountain. Climbing it definitely wouldn't be a joke. A great deal of energy and wisdom would be required to successfully make it through the mountain. The mission was truly getting close to impossible for the man who didn't have ropes. He stopped momentarily at the foot of the mountain as he wandered from one thought to another. The man who made ropes brought them out and immediately tied them around his waist and started climbing the mountain. The colleague had no rope and couldn't therefore do anything. He was so foolish that he refused to make ropes with his friend when they were still in the forest. Where they had reached, there wasn't any reliable tree from which he could make ropes. There was hence no way he could climb the mountain as his friend had made ropes which were not enough for both of them. Consequently, he then made a U-turn and went back to the village.

His wise colleague managed to climb the mountain and eventually went on to tour the land which fortunately had exactly what it was believed to be having. Gold, silver, diamond, mercury and other resources were in plenty on top of the land being extremely fertile. In fact, the man had never before seen or heard of any land being as fertile as that one. He later went back to his village and reported to the king all that he saw. The king went on to conquer the land. The wise man was rewarded by the king just as they were promised at the beginning. The foolish man however, never got anything as he gave up on the way. The king was instead very furious with him for what he did. He therefore wasted his time and energy. He was even relieved of his spying role for the kingdom; his position was given to another man.

Now what do we learn from this story? We all set out to do things in life but not all of us persist until we accomplish them. Like the foolish man, many people do not plan early enough to overcome challenges in life. Consequently, they give up on their goals when they encounter challenges. The men clearly saw the challenge which was the mountain that was on the way. They would have to climb it in order to continue with their journey. What they wanted was exactly on the other side of it. For them to achieve their targets, they had to first go through the challenge before them. The foolish man didn't collect the resources necessary to climb the mountain but slackened off upon seeing it. He wanted to first reach it; little did he know that it would only get bigger as they approached it. That's poor planning.

He reached there only to realize that it was a very big mountain, bigger than what he had imagined. Therefore, he couldn't go forward as he didn't have what to use for climbing the mountain. He had not properly planned for the great challenge. Foolishness cost him all the benefits he was destined to get after accomplishing the task. Giving up on one task made him lose everything including even his position in the kingdom. Yet if he had been wise, he would have done just like his friend.

He thus chased the wind in the name of working so hard to achieve his targets. He risked his precious life for nothing and at the end lost everything while his wise friend, who persevered, gained everything. When they saw the mountain covering the road, he gathered what he would need to climb it. That is wisdom. He could have done just like his foolish counterpart, yet he chose to be different. He tried to persuade his friend to do the same unfortunately he had a weak mindset which couldn't get him forward in the midst of the difficulties they were facing.

Many people are like the foolish man; they start doing something very well but along the way, they encounter challenges and give up yet what they need could be on the other side of the challenges before them. Failure to successfully navigate through their challenges causes them to eventually fail to get what they set out for. Their mindsets are so weak that they cannot persist through their challenges. They focus more on the challenges they face than their goals. With the wrong mindset, you can never achieve your goals. To accomplish your targets, you have to endure all the difficulties you meet on the way. You have to realize that challenges are prerequisites for success. If you shy away from them, you will never succeed. You have to go through them first before you can achieve what you want.

Proper planning is required if you must overcome your difficulties and achieve your targets. People with weak mindsets, cannot navigate through the storms of life. They end up chasing the wind in the name of working so hard just like the foolish man. Giving up quickly comes to the minds of such people whenever they encounter challenges of whatever nature. They quit and hence never win. They fail to control their challenges due to poor planning; instead they allow their challenges to control them. Failing to plan is planning to fail.

Unlike the foolish man, the wise man was more than determined to accomplish the task. Nothing whatsoever could make him quit. He never focused on the challenges he encountered; he focused on his goals which were bigger than all the challenges he faced. He was willing to do all he could in order to achieve his goals. He reached the mountain when he was fully prepared to climb it having made ropes from the trees in the forest. He had a strong mindset that kept him going through all the challenges. No wonder he eventually succeeded and was greatly rewarded. He fought a good fight and he finished the race; behold he was crowned by the king. He ran till he crossed the finishing line. As they were about to reach the village, they faced their greatest challenge-the huge mountain.

The race is toughest when you are about to cross the finishing line; there you have to be extraordinarily careful otherwise you will fail to cross that line. In a race, only those who cross the finishing line are crowned. If you don't cross that line, you can't get a number. The one who takes the first position in a race is the first person to cross the finishing line.

The wise man crossed that line and was definitely rewarded. There is no reward for those who start and stop on the way like the foolish man. If anything, they lose a lot as their efforts can likely be futile. They end up wasting time and energy just because of giving up on the way.

You can choose to be either the wise man or foolish man. You can choose either to give up or persevere. How many tasks have you started but you gave up on the way because you didn't plan as required? Can you imagine how much time and energy you have wasted by giving up on the way? Do you have the right mindset for achieving your targets? Do you easily quit when things get tough or endure till the end? Do you focus more on your challenges or goals?

What have you set out to accomplish? What mountain do you anticipate on the way? How are you planning for it? Are you gathering what you will need to climb it or you first want to get to the spot on which it is located and find out its nature? What you need is on the other side of the mountain. If you don't climb it, you won't get it. To climb it, you need the necessary resources which you have to gather before reaching the mountain. If you don't plan properly, then it might be hard for you to get what you want. You may not gather all you will need as you may not know how big the mountain is but at least get what you can; that is proper planning. It is better to reach there when you have something and realize you are lacking certain things than when you have absolutely nothing to even start with.

You have to plan properly if you must go forward when faced with difficulties. You must lay proper strategies to achieve your goals in life depending on the situation and available resources. Evaluate your progress, and adjust where necessary and above all, believe in yourself that you can achieve the goals. Be willing to go the extra mile; to persist even when everyone else gives up. Most people usually give up on the premise that something is impossible to do. Well, it may be impossible for them but not you. It could actually be your gift. Just because they can't do it doesn't necessarily mean you too can't. If you listen to them, you will end up losing just like them. Such people surrender when things get tough. Whenever they fail to accomplish a task, they are very quick to justify their laziness and failure.

The foolish man didn't climb the mountain because he did not collect what he would need to climb it due to his laziness and foolishness which made it hard for him to plan properly. Otherwise he had the ability to climb it. He gave up on the premise that there was a huge mountain on the way that made it impossible for him to achieve his target. Only his fellow lazy people would believe him. They would understand since they have similar mindsets with which they would actually do just like he did. They wouldn't even bother to ask him about his friend who went on to climb the mountain. They would say the wise man was just lucky. But the king didn't believe him. He got the shock of his life when the king instead demoted him from his spy position. The king surely had a very distinctive mindset. He realized that the wise man was able to climb the mountain and reach the land and survey it.

The foolish man could have persevered as well. Only that he focused on the challenges not the goals. The wise man however focused on the goals. He eventually made it and got his rewards. If the king had the mindset of the foolish man, he would understand him as they did not leave the palace with anything to help them in climbing any mountain. However, even though the mountain was not even the least of what the two men expected on the way, the king didn't condone whatever the foolish man told him.

Some challenges are invisible at the beginning; you meet them along the way but you have to quickly strategize so that you overcome them. Achieving your targets requires you to be flexible. You will most likely give up in life if you are not flexible. Quite often things do not work out according to your original plan. You have to adjust accordingly so that you successfully go through all the difficulties you face. Flexibility is one of the most powerful recipes for success. Every successful person out there will tell you that they adjusted many times along the way to reach where they are. To successful people giving up is not an option. They don't quit but adjust when they face challenges. They know that the pain they go through as they pursue their goals is only temporary. They are never discouraged but inspired by their challenges.

When they encounter challenges, they aren't too quick to call for help from other people; they plan on how best to overcome them. They are sacrificial, resilient, determined, hardworking and persistent; they have the right attitude and they believe in themselves. They do not listen to negative-minded people, never give excuses, never fear failing, think outside the box and in the future, take necessary risks, make proper choices, motivate themselves to go on even when there is no one to motivate them; they are open-minded not rigid, willing to stay awake when everyone else is asleep.

They think to find the solutions to their problems; they don't cry over spilled milk but think to refill the empty milk container. They start doing something with the end in mind-they know from the beginning, what exactly they want to achieve at the end and fix their eyes on it. They pay the extra price to go the extra mile. That is why they get ahead of others. If you really want to achieve your targets in life, then do like them. They are not any superior; they just know what they want and how to get it. They further know that the rewards are greater than the challenges they meet on the way. They therefore plan properly and end up achieving their targets.

What are you willing to sacrifice to achieve your goals? What price are you willing to pay to get what you want? Are you ready to make ropes for climbing the mountain before you? Do not ever give up on your goals no matter what you encounter along the way. Great people emerge through crises. Embrace your challenges and you will emerge a champion just like the wise man. Keep focused on the rewards not the challenges. You may never discover that you can overcome a particular challenge until you face it. You may never realize how strong you are until you are hit by a storm. For every success attained, there is a price paid. Everyone wants to succeed in life but not everybody is willing to pay the price. Success is not a happenstance; it is a systematic process. You do not just simply wake up one morning and succeed with no efforts put.

Do not be like the foolish man but the wise one. It is just a matter of choice to be like either of the two. Make a proper choice; choose to be like the wise man. You can climb the mountain before you and achieve your goals. Pursue them with all your might. You will be greatly rewarded for your efforts. Fear not the mountain and let it not intimidate you regardless of how big it is. Whatever you fear will subdue you. You are stronger than you can ever imagine.

Do not limit your potential by thinking negatively. Be a positive thinker in all circumstances. That way, you will be in a proper position to achieve your targets. You might have given up on something you were doing. I challenge you to try it again but with a different mindset-that it's possible to succeed in it. I guarantee you the outcome will be totally different this time.

That which you gave up on doing could lead to your breakthrough in life. Do not believe that you have already failed. Perhaps you just gave up when things became tough yet you were about to cross over and get what you wanted. Maybe you quit because someone said you would not succeed and you listened to them; you were therefore surrounded by the wrong people and hence the environment was not favorable for you to achieve your goals. Maybe you feared you could fail. Or perhaps you had not gathered what you needed to overcome your challenges just like the foolish man. It could also be that your goals were not clear or you did not have them at all. Hence you ended up chasing the wind as you did not know exactly what you wanted and thus could not strategize carefully to achieve it. You were therefore at the mercy of the challenges you met on the way which consequently sealed your fate. You unconsciously allowed them to devour your goals.

Your goals are so precious that you should never permit the challenges you encounter to kill them. Your challenges are only as big as you perceive them to be. To the wise man, the mountain appeared smaller than his targets. He went on to climb it and meet his targets. To the foolish man, the mountain was bigger than his targets. He therefore gave up on his targets. The land they had gone to survey was just on the other side of the mountain. They could achieve their targets only after climbing the mountain. In other words, climbing the mountain was the prerequisite for achieving their targets.

Climb the mountain before you. What you want is on the other side of it. To get it, you must first climb the mountain. If you give up, you will miss it. You will have wasted a lot of time and energy. You came from far; do not afford to give up now. Persist a little more; you will soon get what you want and your story will change just like that of the wise man. In whatever you do, endeavor to always plan properly.

CHAPTER SIX
FAILURE IS NOT THE END

In the second semester of my third year at Makerere University, there was a course unit called Product Design and Development. It covers how to come up with a product right from scratch to the consumer. It is very wide as the stages involved in developing a product are numerous. The lecturer used to give us progressive group assignments starting with identifying a product that each group of students would develop throughout the semester. For each of the topics covered, there would be an assignment which would be an addition to the previous ones. The first assignment was only to identify the product of choice of each group of students. In the second assignment, the actual work of developing the product commenced.

The assignments were progressive in a sense that one would lead to the next one. The order of the assignments was the order of the topics in the course unit. If you failed one, you wouldn't proceed to do the next one. You would have to first correct the one you failed. Each of the assignments was marked out of 40. In the second assignment, my group scored only 15 out of 40. It was the worst of all the groups. It was the first time at the university that my group was the worst in an assignment. We had failed the assignment terribly. We would have to redo it in order to be able to proceed to do the third one. Definitely, we did not like the results.

When the results were released, all my group members gathered to discuss and review ours. Our target was to find out why we got that little mark. We looked back to find out what could have gone wrong. Starting from the beginning, each of the members had to explain exactly how they did their parts of the assignment-where they got information from, how they researched, what else they were doing while carrying out the work and many others. We discovered we made a lot of mistakes that cost us marks. We had to lay proper strategies of how to avoid those mistakes in the proceeding assignments.

We were not discouraged by the 15 we got; we worked even harder than before in the subsequent assignments. We prayed harder, stayed awake later than before and researched more than we did before; consulted wider than before and read more than before. In a nutshell, we became more serious. We told ourselves that each of us had to make it a point that we had to not just pass but excel in all the remaining assignments. We set for our group new targets which we would all strive tooth and nail to achieve. We set out to work for 40 out of 40 in the remaining assignments and nothing less than that. We collectively decided we would never fail again. The 15 we got was an eye-opener to the reality that we had to wake up. We made mistakes which we learnt from.

We committed ourselves to doing the work. We believed we could get much more than the 15 we got. We told ourselves that even though our group was the worst, we were not the worst. We believed there was a place at the top for us; we only would have to pay the price to claim it. We accepted our results and decided to take full responsibility. From that point, we never settled for what we had as we were always hungry for more marks.

With the unwavering zeal we developed, not even 40 out of 40 in the assignments would satisfy us. With the new strategies we laid, our results definitely changed. We started scoring highly in the proceeding assignments, mostly 38 out of 40, the maximum the lecturer ever gave. Each time the results came back, we would congratulate ourselves and say to one another something like, "Great work dear. Glory be to God! We made it. Now that this assignment is done, let's focus on the next one and do even more. This is not our best; we can still get better than it. We are the best and nothing less than that. Let's ceaselessly run the race till we cross the finishing line."

We really worked hard in the course unit and in the end; I and one other person scored 'A' while the rest of the members also scored highly. Our group was the overall best out of all the groups. With our determination, hard work, perseverance, resilience, faith and hope, we made it from the worst to the best, from failure to success; to the surprise of our classmates and even the lecturer himself.

We all fail in life quite often. But how do we respond to failure? What do you do when you miss your targets? Do you quit or continue? Do you despair or keep hopeful?

When you fall down, you shouldn't remain there but get up and move on. When life hits you hard, don't give up; hit back and move on. You may need to change your strategies to get different results. Sometimes you have to first fall down to learn how to walk more carefully; you may have to first fail in order to succeed. In fact, failure at one step in life should pave way to success at the next step.

When a child is learning to walk, they fall down several times. As they fall, they learn to walk more carefully. They don't give up on walking just because they fall the first, second, or third time they try. The more they fall, the more they walk. They are so curious to discover what is at the next step that they are still willing to try again irrespective of how badly they fall. This keeps them focused ahead. Yes, they sometimes cry or even get injured when they fall but they still get up and continue walking. Nothing ever makes them quit walking. A time comes when they master the art of walking and graduate from walking to running.

No one is born walking; we all learn to walk. As we learn, we fall down yet we don't resign but press on. We pay the price to learn to walk. That's what you should do when you don't meet your targets in life. When you fail to achieve something, examine the circumstances that led to your failure so that you don't fail in a similar manner again. If you made a mistake that caused you to fail, you will not repeat that mistake. It's not a bad thing to fail to accomplish something as long as you have a positive mindset; in fact, it's normal to fail. Failure is not final as long as you are willing to press on. It should actually motivate you to work even harder than before.

The 15 which we got in our second assignment was a stepping stone to our excellence in the course unit. We never allowed it to discourage us in any way. We had the winning attitude which kept us fighting till the end. Failing in life doesn't necessarily mean someone is a failure. Even though we failed the assignment, we never considered ourselves to be failures. We put in more efforts and later achieved great results which were motivated by our failure in the second assignment.

Many people get discouraged whenever they fail; this makes them abandon that which could have led to their breakthrough in life. Still some people fully blame others whenever they fail. They take them to be completely responsible for their failures. But the truth of the matter is that they could have caused their own failures. Some of them might have even contributed the most towards their failures. Even though they may not be fully responsible, they at least carry part of the blame.

When we failed our assignment, we didn't hastily blame others but examined the situation and found out that we caused our own failure. However, even though that was the case, we never condemned any of us. We instead acknowledged our individual contributions and each of us took complete responsibility with immediate effect.

When you fail, start with yourself, not other people. First examine yourself thoroughly before you examine others. Even when you are sure they caused your failure, first find out if in any way you also contributed. When you do that, you will better position yourself to succeed. Blaming others for your failure only paves way for more failures; in fact, it is a sign that you are an irresponsible person. Most of those who blame others after failing hardly succeed in life. As you examine yourself after failing, be careful not to judge or condemn yourself.

Otherwise, you might be disappointed in yourself. It will then be very difficult for you to recollect yourself and continue pursuing what you want. You should always be positive about yourself even after suffering from what to you might be the greatest failure. When you have the right mindset, you can always press on even if you suffer defeats in life. Failure only delays success; it doesn't stop it.

Sometimes life hits you and you fall down; however, you have to get up and keep moving. Never remain down; be resilient enough to carry on. Failure should never be a reason to give up at any point in life. It doesn't seal your fate as long as you are willing to press on. Never be discouraged when you fail. There's always a lot you can achieve after failing.

Sir Winston Leonard Spencer Churchill (1874-1965) said "Success is not final; failure is not fatal. It's the courage to continue that counts." Yes, the courage to continue matters a lot. Are you courageous enough to continue when you fail in something? If you don't move on, you will fail to attain the success that lies ahead of you. Life doesn't end where you are; there's a lot more in the future. If you choose to stay where you are, you will always lag behind. Life is not static and never ever will it be. You just have to be dynamic for it to accommodate you.

Success will never lower its standards to accommodate you; you have to raise yours to attain it. To succeed in life, you need to know how to handle failure. If you fail to manage failure, then you will hardly succeed. Failing today is no indication that you will fail forever. Marilyn Monroe (1926-1962) said, "Just because you fail once, it does not mean you are going to fail at everything. Keep trying, hold on, and always, always, always believe in yourself because if you don't, then who will? So keep your head high, keep your chin up, and most importantly, keep smiling because life is a beautiful thing and there is so much to smile about."

You may fail in something today and excel in another tomorrow. If you allow failure at one thing to discourage you from moving on, you will fail to succeed in the next thing. If you permit the failure of today to discourage you, then you will not attain the success of tomorrow. Today's failure doesn't necessarily seal tomorrow's fate. You should be hopeful that success will come even though you fail. Sometimes the darkest moment is proceeded by the brightest one. You shouldn't therefore despair even at the biggest failure you suffer. In every situation in life, you must not only be hopeful always but as well keep the hope alive. Life loses meaning when you lose hope.

The moment you lose hope, you will quit. And most people lose hope even when they encounter the slightest failure. This makes it very difficult for them to have clear visions for their lives as they are often thinking they will fail. This stops them from pursuing their dreams when things get tough as they will have nothing to motivate them. Your vision motivates you to move on even though you fail. To develop a clear vision for your life, you shouldn't be thinking of failure.

Failing today doesn't necessarily mean you will succeed tomorrow; you may still fail. However, always focus on success not failure. Focusing on success will keep you working hard to attain it. I love this life-transforming statement made by Roy T. Bennett that, "Failure is a bend in the road, not the end of the road. Learn from failure and keep moving forward." Not many people learn from failure. That's why they can hardly succeed after failing.

They permit failure to seal their fates. Some people believe they are very unlucky. Others claim they were born at the wrong time, in the wrong place and by the wrong parents.

These and many more limiting beliefs hinder them from attaining success. To such people, failure is always inevitable. Whenever they fail in something, they turn to their ill-fated beliefs for consolation instead of thinking differently so as to achieve different results. Failure will stop you from succeeding only when you permit it. Sometimes you must first fail today to prepare yourself to succeed tomorrow. In fact, some of the greatest successes ever recorded in the world were realized after calamitous failures. Some of the people the world today reveres as highly successful first failed miserably before they made it. Let's have a look at five of them.

A.   Abraham Lincoln. 'Born in 1809, he was a champion of equal rights, and he blazed a trail towards the freedom of slaves in America. He failed numerous times in his life. In 1832 at the age of 23, he lost his job. At the same time, he also lost his bid for State Legislature. Just 3 years later at the age of 26, the love of his life, Ann Rutledge died. Another three years later, he lost his bid to become the Speaker in the Illinois House of Representatives. In 1848, at the age of 39, Lincoln also failed in his bid to become Commissioner of the General Land office in D.C Washington. Ten years later, at 49, he was defeated at his quest to become a U.S Senator. But he never gave up. In 1846, he was elected to the U.S House of Representatives where he drafted a bill to abolish slavery. At the age of 52 in 1861, he was elected the 16th president of the United States of America. Lincoln failed several times but never gave up on his dreams. He persisted amidst all the challenges he went through. Failing numerous times was not enough to make him quit'[1]. One of his quotes is this: "Be sure you put your feet in the right place then stand firm."

B.   Albert Einstein. 'Born in 1879, he is known as one of the most brilliant minds to have ever lived on

---

[1] www.wanderlustworker.com

earth. He is one of the greatest scientists of all time. Einstein was once considered a major failure. He never spoke until he was four years old. In 1895, at the age of sixteen, he failed to pass the examination for entrance into the prestigious Swiss Federal Polytechnic School located in Zurich, Switzerland; though he did outstandingly well in physics and mathematics, he failed the non-science subjects, doing especially badly in French so he wasn't accepted.

In that same year, he continued his studies at the Cantonal School of Aargau in Aarau, Switzerland; he studied well and this time, he passed the entry exams into the Swiss Federal Polytechnic School. So the next year, at seventeen, he finally started studying at the school. While he did graduate from the University of Zurich, he struggled and nearly dropped out, doing very poorly during the course of his studies there. He was in such a dire state that at the time of his father's death, he considered his son to be a major failure, which left young Albert completely heartbroken. After graduating, he wandered, unsure of what to do with his life. After some time, he ended up taking a job as an insurance salesman, going door to door in an attempt to sell insurance.

Eventually two years later, he took a job at the patent office as an assistant examiner, evaluating patent applications for variety of devices. He later brought the theory of relativity, with groundbreaking work done in Mathematics and Physics. He developed several fundamental laws governing Physics and created the beginning of the Quantum theory. In 1921, he won the Nobel Prize. He once said, "Everybody is a genius. But if you judge a fish by its ability to climb a tree, it will live its whole life believing that it is stupid.""[2]

C.   Michael Jeffrey Jordan. 'He is a former professional basketball player. He is considered one of the greatest basketball players of all time. Jordan was born in 1963. At the age of 15, while at Emsley A. Laney high school in Wilmington, he tried out for the varsity Basketball team during his sophomore year but the head coach Clifton "Pop" Herring claimed he was too short to play at that level. There were 15 roster spots but Jordan failed to get one; his close friend Sophomore Leroy Smith did.

Jordan went home, locked himself in his room and cried. "It was embarrassing not making the team," Jordan later said in 1991, "they posted the roster and it was there for a long, long time without my name on it." After failing to make the varsity team, Jordan was assigned to the junior team. He picked himself up and turned his

---

[2] www.wanderlustworker.com, www.physicsoftheuniverse.com and www.abc.net.au

omission from the varsity team into his motivation to succeed in Basketball. Determined to prove his worth, he became the star of Laney's junior varsity team and tallied several 40 plus-point games and attracted crowds that were unprecedented for a junior varsity affair. Failure never discouraged him; it made him strive harder to excel.

"Whenever I was working out and got tired and figured I ought to stop, I'd close my eyes and see that list in the locker room without my name on it," Jordan would explain, "that usually got me going again."

At 21, he joined the National Basketball Association (NBA) as a professional basketball player for the Chicago Bulls. He had many achievements including, but not limited to the following: winning six championship titles, three in a row, two times (1991-1993 and 1996-1998), being the NBA scoring champion ten times and winning the NBA's Most Valuable Player Award five times. He is one of the most impactful basketball players to ever grace the courts. On his success, Jordan is quoted to have said, "I've missed more than 9000 shots in my career. I've lost more than 300 games. 26 times, I have been trusted to take the game winning shot and missed. I've failed over and over and over again in my life. And that's why I succeed."'[3]

D.   Henry Ford. 'He is known for the Ford Motor Company, one of the most successful automotive companies of all time. However, he failed two times before that led to bankruptcies, prior to his success. He is no stranger to failure yet he never gave up. In 1899, at the age of 36, he formed his first company, the Detroit Automobile Company with backing from the famed lumber baron, William H. Murphy. In 1901, that company went bankrupt and ceased operations.

He made his second attempt that same year, when he formed the Henry Ford Company, which he ended up leaving with the rights to his name. That company was later renamed to the Cadillac Automobile Company. It was in 1903, at the age of 40 that he succeeded. He incorporated the Ford Motor Company. He revolutionized the automobile industry. He went from failure to success.'[4] He once said, "Failure is simply the opportunity to begin again, this time more intelligently."

E.   Thomas Alva Edison. 'This famous American made 10,000 unsuccessful attempts to invent a

---

[3] www.uky.edu, www.wanderlustworker.com, www.newsweek.com and Newsweek Special Edition; Jordan, 30 years since MJ changed the game.
[4] way4vision.wordpress.com, www.cbsnews.com and www.wanderlustworker.com

commercially viable incandescent electric light bulb but he never gave up. When a reporter asked him, "How did it feel to fail 10,000 times?" Edison replied "I didn't fail 10,000 times. The light bulb was an invention with 10,000 steps." This is also the same person whose teachers said was "too stupid to learn anything," and was fired from his first two positions for "not being productive". He is someone who refused to ever give up no matter what happened. One of his quotes is that, "Many of life's failures are people who did not realize how close they were to success when they gave up.""[5]

* * * * * *

There are numerous individuals who first dreadfully failed in life but later went on to become very successful. Their names became synonymous with success. Not all of them can be noted here. However, from the above examples, it's clear that we shouldn't quit when we fail. We should not be discouraged by failure; we should instead be encouraged by it to push harder to achieve better results. Never give up on your dreams after suffering a defeat. Never believe that you aren't good, smart, and talented or gifted enough to succeed in life. Some people throw in the towel in life when they are about to succeed. Some give up at the ninth attempt when they are destined to succeed in the tenth one.

---

[5] www.uky.edu and www.wanderlustworker.com, How to sell you way through life, Napoleon Hill, John Wiley & Sons, Inc, 2010.

Consequently, they miss their opportunities to succeed. Don't ever be one of such people. When you fail, find out why and how it happened. Get back when you are stronger and more prepared to succeed. Failure shouldn't deter you from pursuing your dreams. You can still make it even though you fail in something. Everybody fails in life at least at some point; it's not failure that matters but how we handle it.

Management of failure at a particular stage in life is crucial for success at the next one. The difference between those who fail once and never succeed and those who fail but later succeed lies in their management of failure. The former do not know how to manage failure. They don't believe in themselves. They think they are not good enough to make it. They are not determined and often give up when they fail. They lack the winning attitude and their mindsets are too weak to keep them moving on whenever they miss their targets in life. To them, failure is the end of the road. Once they fail, they believe it's done. When they fall down, they choose to stay down; they never bother to rise up and continue pursuing their interests.

They want the whole world to know that they have fallen down. They cry as loud as they can whenever hit by the storms of life. They end up failing even more. One failure breeds another.

The latter however, know how to manage failure. They are never discouraged by it. They work even harder after failing. They believe they can still make it no matter how badly they fail. They have the winning attitude. They keep striving for what is ahead of them. They pride not in what they have already succeeded at, but what they want to succeed in. They are positive-minded and determined to succeed. They don't give up on their dreams but pursue them relentlessly. If you should succeed after failing, then you need to be one of such people. When you fail in a particular thing, focus on the next one that you want to succeed in not the one which you have already failed in.

Develop the right mindset that keeps you moving even if you fail. Don't be quick to think of quitting when your success could be at the next attempt. Never permit failure to daunt you from attaining your success. Failure is just a bend in the path of success. When you fall down, rise up and move on. Your success lies ahead of you. When you resign, you will miss it. Count on your possibilities of success not failure. Don't make failure your project. Nobody was created to be a failure; we choose what we become. You can either become a success or failure depending on what you choose to do with your life.

Failing at something doesn't necessarily make you a failure; it's by choice that you become a failure. You can either make this choice consciously or unconsciously.

Choose to succeed even when you fail. Success won't happen unless you make it happen. Make your success, not failure, happen.

CHAPTER SEVEN
FIND YOUR NICHE IN THE WORLD

Whenever people hear the name Leonel Messi, football comes to their minds. When the name Floyd Mayweather Jr. is mentioned, boxing immediately comes to people's minds. The name Job Lazarus Okello is synonymous with inspiration and motivation. Sir Isaac Newton? Well, this great man is known for his revolutionary works in Science. The list is long. What about you? What comes to people's minds when they hear or read your name? What do people know you for? What is it that you do that moves others? How have you branded yourself? What is it that is synonymous with your name? What defines you?

Everybody has a unique niche in the world; no one is a mistake or an accident. The onus is on each of us to find our respective niches. Your niche is next to your name; in fact, it's your silent last name. *WordWeb* dictionary defines the word niche as *"a position particularly well suited to the person who occupies it."* Everyone has a position in life which they should occupy. Most people occupy the wrong positions in life that's why they struggle so hard yet do not achieve what they set out for.

You can't excel in life when you are in the wrong niche. Some people could be the greatest writers in the world if only they put thoughts on papers and put the papers together into books; yet they don't know that they have fortes in the writing world. Some of those who could sing the greatest songs are busy listening to other people's songs not knowing that they have slots in the music fraternity. Other people are supposed to come up with great scientific inventions yet there are unaware of their places in the science world.

Some of the greatest leaders are being led by other people simply because they haven't found their niches in the leadership realm. I have ever heard people praising certain products that they are so exceptional. Some of those people could actually be the best product developers if only they could realize they have their niches in the domain of product development.

We all have our spheres of excellence and influence in the world yet not many people have found theirs. Irrespective of who you are, how you are, where you are coming from, what you have and `what you do, there's a distinguished place for you in the world. You have to find and ultimately exploit it. Don't just admire people for what they are, where they are, what they have and what they do or have done; ask yourself "When will I be admired by others?" Don't only enjoy other people's products; develop something as well.

Those whose products that you enjoy put in a lot of efforts to develop them. They found their niches in the product development world. Don't only go around singing other people's names; when will your name be in the lips of others for something they know you for? Those whose names are prominent found their niches in the world and established themselves in them. If you haven't found your area of influence in the world, then you might be sleeping too much, relaxing beyond normal, or perhaps not reading and researching enough, not using your mind well and wasting too much time pursuing useless things. In your niche, you are very influential; you can't be disregarded by other people. There are so many people in the world today, of different cultures and colors, from different backgrounds and living in different parts of the world; each of them with a distinguished place in the world.

Let nobody deceive you that you are useless in any way; you are very special. There is a place for everyone in the world. The fact that your niche is different from that of others does not necessarily mean you are a mediocre. Become so good in an area that people can easily find and can't ignore you in it. In your niche, you are the master of your game. Great things are done by people who have found their niches and have established themselves in them. People like Sir Isaac Newton, Dr. Myles Munroe, Nelson Mandela, Job Lazarus Okello, Albert Einstein, Thomas Edison, Donald Trump and Abraham Lincoln among others all found their respective niches.

You do not necessarily have to do what they have done. Your niche might not be in the world of science, politics, music, invention, academic and business among others. Whatever your niche is, you have to find and trail it. Therefore, stop focusing on other people's lives. Find your niche and establish yourself in it. You may not have to do very big things in order to write your part of history. There are little things you can do in your niche that the world can't get rid of. Whatever you do in your niche will always make you stand out.

Are things not moving on well for you? Are you struggling with life where you are? Do you ever feel like you are living in the wrong place in the world? You are not alone and it's not a crime to feel that way. A lot of people worldwide believe they are living in the wrong countries; they greatly admire other countries. They think that life would be better if they were in the countries of their dreams. But the real issue is that they don't know their niches.

As a matter of fact, your country might be the best place for you to flourish. If you leave it, you may fail to find your niche. Though you may need to be in another place or country to develop in your niche, you don't necessarily have to leave your country in order to find it. You can discover your niche right where you are. Have you tried out many things but can't find where exactly you fit? Do you wander from one sphere of life to another but can't find where you belong?

Well, find out the position from which you are operating and what you are doing. Maybe you are in the wrong niche. Just like every plant flourishes best in a particular kind of soil, so do you thrive best in your niche. It is that particular position you are meant to hold in the world in a given realm of life. It is your domain of influence. There is something you can always do to change the world; it's in your niche that you can best do it.

There is a particular field in life in which each of us flourishes best. Nelson Mandela found his niche in the leadership world, Messi in football, Mayweather in boxing, Michael Jordan in Basketball, many examples can be given here. Therefore, it is paramount that each of us finds out our respective spheres of influence. It will be very difficult for other people to intimidate or manipulate you when you know your niche and have fully established yourself in it. Nobody will belittle or make you feel inferior in any way. You will have a high self-esteem and will be proud of yourself. You will see yourself as an asset to the world. You will have big dreams, visions and goals in life and ceaselessly chase them.

If you know your niche, let no one make you forsake it. Many people will try to discourage you from what you are doing yet that could be in your field of influence. You should thus be very careful and protect your niche. Those who will discourage you from your niche either do not know theirs or are just jealous of you. Those who know theirs and have correct hearts will help you find and/or protect yours; those who know theirs but have evil hearts will make every effort to ensure that you don't find yours or discourage you from it if you already know it.

Search deeply through your heart and discover what you naturally love doing and pursue it wholeheartedly. You will establish yourself in it. You will then occupy a particular place in the world in line with that which you love doing. I naturally love inspiring and motivating people. I do everything I can to make sure I exceptionally carry out this noble task. I do it with all my might and no wonder I found my niche in the realm of inspiration and motivation. This inspirational book is one of the products of the establishment of myself in my niche. Know your niche, establish and develop yourself in it and guard it jealously.

CHAPTER EIGHT
INVEST IN YOURSELF

I once sat in a bus next to a Kenyan lady called Sharon as we travelled from Thika to Nairobi. For most parts of the journey, she was complaining to a friend on phone about how much she hated her life. She told the friend several things but what struck me the most was that she didn't value her life at all.

After she was done talking with her friend, I asked her what she was doing with her life every day to make it better than it was the previous day. Looking greatly astonished, she answered, "My friend, I am a carefree lady; I don't want stress. I go by what life offers me only that I don't love my life." We discussed a lot about life for the rest of the journey. As we talked, I discovered that the lady wasn't investing in the things that would improve her life that's why she didn't love and value her life. Day by day, her life would only worsen. She became frustrated and hopeless as life continually became meaningless to her. She got to understand that it was important for her to invest in her life for it to be meaningful to her. She set out to work on herself so as to improve her life.

A week later, she called me and joyfully said, "...Job, my life has tremendously changed ever since we met in the bus last time. For the first time in my life, I am hopeful and happy. At last life is meaningful to me. I will never be hopeless again. I had been messing up my life because I was too blind to realize that it's very valuable. Since our meeting, I have taken complete responsibility over my life; I won't waste it again. Thanks a lot. May God really bless you..." Our meeting was her turning point; through it, she got to know how she could make her life count.

What are you doing with your life? Do you really like your life? If a movie depicting your life was secretly recorded without your knowledge, would you happily watch that movie? Would you recommend it to other people? Why or why not? Well, it's a fact that for you to value something, you must invest in it. Therefore, invest in your life that you may value it. He who wastes his life hasn't really invested much in it. Are you at school? Do you want to value your education? Invest in it. Those who don't take school seriously haven't sufficiently invested in it. To value your future, invest in it. Whatever you invest in, you'll treasure. Today it's very common to find people drinking the whole day and night thereby failing to fulfill their responsibilities in life. Such people haven't really invested in their lives. They have very peculiar definitions of life.

Invest in your family that you may treasure it. Invest in your parents, children, relatives, friends, but most importantly, invest in yourself; add value to yourself every day. That way, you will make yourself increasingly valuable to the world. Don't waste your life as if you borrowed it from someone. Nobody should treasure your life more than yourself. You have never lived this day before and you will never live it again; therefore, make the most of it. Today is yet another day in your life; make it count more than the past days of your life. Invest heavily in your life today. The world is very unforgiving to those who joke with their lives. Many people have died because they played with their lives. Their irresponsible behaviors cost them their dear lives.

Work on yourself to become better every day. The only person I compete with today is the person I was yesterday. I strive to be a better person today than I was yesterday. I am so conscious of this that at the beginning of each day, I plan what I want to do with my life that day and at the end of the day, I examine myself to see if I did all I wanted to do and how my life was affected. I analyse if I am better or worse than the previous day. This enables me to know how to better my life. What about you? How do you live your day?

Make a difference with your life every day. Don't permit into your life whatever destroys it. The world over, a lot of people are wasting their lives or even dying altogether just because they allowed into their lives what is destructive. For example, many people today are succumbing to lung cancer which they got through smoking; alcoholism is also seriously claiming lives today and ruining the lives of many people; still many people are getting ruined through immoral acts like prostitution, defilement and rape among others. Numerous examples can be cited here.

It's your responsibility to invest in your life, to be watchful over and protect it. Your life is so precious that you should guard it jealously. Do at least something that makes you a better person every day. Let the world see the values you are adding to your life. You will be admired and honored for that. Investment in yourself is one of the greatest and most precious investments you can ever make. Read life-transforming books, attend seminars, conferences, prayer meetings and fellowships among other things and acquire knowledge and skills, to discover and develop yourself. Create demand for yourself by investing in your life. Be a person of positive substances.

Be very mindful of what you listen to, watch and read. Not every song, video or book is good for you; others can ruin your life. Likewise, not every function is good for you. I have seen people whose lives worsened after reading certain materials, watching certain movies, listening to certain songs and attending certain functions. What do you listen to? What do you watch? What do you read? What kind of functions do you attend? You should be very selective; go for only what adds values to your life. Before you do something, ask yourself; "How will it add value to my life?" In other words, how better will you be after doing it? If it won't improve your life, then don't do it.

If you are not selective, then you will go for just anything life offers. Consequently, your life will be ruined as not everything you will go for will be good. If you invest negatively in your life, you will attain negative results. Good can never come out of bad. Bad is bad and will always be. To get good results, invest in the right things, at the right time, in the right place with the right people. In life, not everything is meant for everyone; and not every opportunity suits everyone. You can't invest in everything or everybody and excel in life; you have to be selective in whatever you do.

If you don't utilize your life well today, you might fail to be the person you are meant to be tomorrow. Some people are meant to be the leaders of tomorrow, others teachers, doctors, lawyers, engineers, accountants and entrepreneurs among others but that may not happen if they waste their lives today. Wasting life is simultaneous with wasting opportunities. If you waste your life, you might miss the opportunity to become that person you're meant to become. Everyone has something which they can do best. To ultimately do it, they have to invest in their life; they should make it count.

You may waste your life once but end up crying for the rest of it. If you venture into whatever you don't need at any particular time, the end results will always be disastrous. If you are a student, pursue your studies tenaciously till completion. Be fully a student; don't chase anything else other than books. Whatever won't positively contribute to your success, don't do it. There is time for everything. You can't do many things at the same time and excel equally in all of them. Jesus Christ put it beautifully as recorded in the scriptures in Matthew 6:24 (NIV) that, *"No one can serve two masters. Either he will hate the one and love the other, or he will be devoted to the one and despise the other. You cannot serve both God and Money."*

If you are a teacher, give yourself to teaching and building of people and consequently shaping their future; be their fountain of knowledge. Invest in building students into responsible and productive people. Keep focused on that. Don't be selfish with your knowledge; pour it out to others. You have it, they need it. Your knowledge is useless to the society if you keep it only to yourself. You didn't study only for yourself but for others as well.

Use your knowledge to transform the world. A doctor should wholeheartedly concentrate on treating patients, restoring their hopes and putting smiles on their faces even in hard situations. A Christian has a great call of preaching the gospel and winning the lost to Jesus Christ; they should sacrifice everything for the sake of the gospel. An engineer, entrepreneur, accountant and everyone else has their idiosyncratic missions on earth. Know yours and ultimately invest in it.

However, that will happen only when you invest in yourself first. Use your time to invest in yourself. Don't spend time pursuing things that don't build you into a better person. Time is limited therefore make proper use of it. Any time spent doing things that don't add value to your life is a wasted time. To appropriately invest in yourself, you need to manage time properly. Many people often procrastinate because they think they always have time for doing something.

The truth of the matter is that you may have only one opportunity for doing something. Certain opportunities may come but only once in your lifetime; procrastinators are often poised to miss such opportunities. Most of such people are lazy, disorganized and care less enough about their own affairs. They can hardly get things done on time and can't seem to figure out why; they end up losing a lot of time which they can never recover.

Are you a procrastinator? How do you spend your time? Can you properly account for all the 24 hours you have in a day? Procrastinators often miss several valuable opportunities in life; in most cases, they get to realize that such opportunities were there after they have already lost them. That's so ridiculous. As said, "time waits for no man"; we have to be strategic and move with it. A simple tip for managing time is here. Take care of the second before you and make the best use of it; sixty seconds will make up a minute, sixty minutes will make up an hour and twenty-four hours will make up a day. That way, you will be productive the whole day. You will invest only in valuable things. Do that every day and see how your life will enormously change. Keep track of how you spend your time. Time is a very precious gift from God; make the most of it. Plan your time properly so that you know how you are spending it; invest it only in productive ventures.

There shall always be a man among men. This is the man who has invested heavily in his life; be that man. You can be a student among students, teacher among teachers, preacher among preachers, doctor among doctors, engineer among engineers, pastor among pastors, father among fathers, mother among mothers, child among children, Christian among Christians and so on. Be unique in whatever you do. It's just a matter of choice and you have the power to make that choice.

In life, people can always show you the way or even walk with you but they can never walk for you. Do you know why? Because it's your responsibility to walk for yourself. Whatever you do, do it responsibly, because it

surely affects your life. Everything you invest in
contributes either positively or negatively to your life.
Whatever doesn't add anything to your life will surely
subtract something from it. Don't invest your resources
in useless ventures. If you must tap that great treasure
hidden inside you, then investment in yourself is a must.

CHAPTER NINE
DO NOT DESPISE SMALL THINGS AND BEGINNINGS

Whenever you start up something, it is usually small and may appear insignificant. The beginning of everything is often unconvincing. It is therefore very easy to despise small things or beginnings. But does starting small ever mean things won't work out for you? Or perhaps hailing from a simple background, an indication that you won't make it in life? History has it that most of the greatest ever achievements had small beginnings. And most, if not all, of the great people of the world all had simple beginnings.

Hence, it's not the size of your beginning that determines your outcome but what you do with that beginning. Likewise, it's not the size of a thing that matters but how it is managed. You don't necessarily need to have rich parents or even come from a wealthy background to become rich and successful as some people made it from abject poverty. Still, it is stunning that some people, who never even saw their parents, also made it in life.

Below are some of the people and undertakings that had small beginnings. Most of us only see how successful some people are but don't really bother to find out how they started and got where they are. Sometimes we wrongly think it was a walk-over for them. The examples below will bring you to the reality that you don't necessarily need to start big in order to make it in life.

A.   Apple. 'In 1976, Steve Wozniak created the first Apple computer. He then teamed up with the late Steve Jobs and Ronald Wayne, to launch Apple Computer Co. from a small garage in Cupertino, California. They started small but became one of the top brands in the realm of computers'[6].

B.   Hewlett-Packard Co. (HP). 'This company was started by Stanford University graduates Bill Hewlett and Dave Packard in 1939 with a very small investment. They launched their company in a garage. The company was incorporated in 1947 and, 10 years later, became a public company. Just like Apple, HP became one of the leading dealers in computers in the world'[7].

C.   Kentucky Fried Chicken (KFC). 'Colonel Harland Sanders (1890-1980) was 62 years old when he began the move towards profiting from his chicken recipe. He held a number of jobs in his early life including, but not limited to the following: working as an insurance salesman and a service station operator in Nicholasville and later North Corbin, Kentucky. At the service station in North Corbin, he would also feed hungry travelers. He eventually moved his operation to a

---

[6] www.americanexpress.com
[7] www.americanexpress.com

restaurant across the street, and featured a fried chicken so notable that he was named a Kentucky colonel in 1935 by the then governor Ruby Laffoon; he was so well-respected that when he lost his official "colonel" certificate, the state and governor Lawrence Winchester Wetherby just decided in 1950 to re-commission him.

So in truth, he was a colonel twice. The title "colonel" was honorary not the military rank. KFC became one of the first chains to go international. By looking around in your city today, you can easily spot out a KFC Restaurant. Powerful as it became, KFC had such a humble beginning'[8].

D.   Jan Koum. 'He co-founded the popular social media application WhatsApp. He was born in a small village near Kiev in Ukraine. Hailing from poverty, Koum's family emigrated to California. He started learning about computers in his spare time. By 18, he had developed impressive skills. He was hired by Yahoo as an infrastructure engineer in 1997 and spent a decade in that industry before recognizing the huge potential of the app industry in 2009 and starting WhatsApp Inc. By 2014, WhatsApp had become enormously popular.

---

[8] www.inc.com

Facebook bought the app in a deal that made Koum a billionaire'[9].

E.   Myself. You might also be interested in knowing something about me. I was born in a war-ravaged region of northern Uganda in Koro village, in a poverty-stricken family. My parents struggled to raise and educate us with their meagre resources. I would sometimes look for my own money for fees and scholastic materials. Not doing that would mean I would have to stay home as my parents couldn't afford to pay school fees for all of us. Sometimes, they even failed to raise school fees for just one of us. I would sometimes spend nearly the whole term looking for school fees and would only go to school in examinations periods. Surprisingly, I would emerge the best in those examinations. My struggle, with my strong reliance on God, yielded fruits.

Towards the end of high school, I was offered a scholarship by Invisible Children, a local nongovernmental organization, after emerging the best student at Ordinary Level in 2011 from St. Mary's College, Lacor and consequently setting a record in that school-first grade (Division I), aggregate 17 for 8. I then joined St. Joseph's College, Layibi in 2012 for Advanced Level and emerged the best science student in 2013 in

---

[9] Bigshorthistory.com

the entire northern part of Uganda, scooping massive 19 points out of 20, thereby setting a new record in the school. In 2014, I was admitted to Makerere University, Uganda's prime academic institution and oldest university, to pursue Bachelor of Science in Mechanical Engineering on government sponsorship. It was a dream-come-true for me. If I had failed to qualify for the sponsorship, then I would hardly ever join the mighty university. I celebrated in tears together with my mother, brothers and sisters when I saw my name on the list of those admitted to the university on government sponsorship.

And what about inspiring, motivating, empowering people and hence transforming the world? Well, I started transforming people's lives as a kid. Before even realizing, I was already doing it. People used to gather around me and I would talk to them starting with my brothers and sisters as well as other people in our home including my parents and relatives, and those in our neighborhood. I would leave no stone unturned in inspiring people from different walks of life. Children and adults all benefitted from my inspirational services.

From home, I took it to school, always encouraging those who thought they wouldn't make it as well as those from similar backgrounds like me. Very important to mention is that even the teachers as well as parents and other stakeholders of the different schools I attended, were greatly inspired by me. I am glad that today, I have a number of people who say things like: "Because of your great encouragements, Job, I made it," "I would have given up if Job hadn't motivated me," "My turning point was when I met Job," "I could have never changed if I hadn't come across Job," "Through Job, my mindset change," "My life was a mess till Job came into it," "My life became meaningful when I met Job," and many others.

I have spoken at various conferences and seminars in different places both locally and internationally. My writings have enormously transformed lives of people. I believe this book is surely inspiring you. I didn't just wake up one morning and decided I would write a book. Before I realized I had to write a book, I was already massively inspiring people. I later realized I needed to put together the inspirational words on papers which would then be amassed into books. And today you are reading one of them. I am not any superior; I also started small.

I discovered that I had a seed of inspiring people. I nurtured it and it germinated into a plant which has since grown and still continues to grow. Many people all over the world have benefitted from what was once a small seed; they are now reaping the fruits. Yet still many people will benefit from what was very small in the beginning. My background didn't limit me from attaining success in life. It instead inspired me to work incessantly hard to excel. This is just an excerpt from my life story. My story is a long one; another book is needed to fully narrate it.

F. And you? You have your story. You know how you started and what transpired along the way. You know the highs and lows of your life's journey.

* * * * * *

So what can we learn from these stories? Everyone's journey to success is different. Everyone must set out to pursue their dreams, even if they have to start as small as they can ever imagine. The above companies all started small but grew to become multibillion-dollar companies.

The people above started very small but succeeded. If you are enthusiastic about an idea, you can start and grow it; as long as you manage it well, it can grow to become one of the biggest and greatest ever in the world. You don't need tons of money to necessarily start. You just have to start with what you have. Fill a gap in the society by creating solutions to the problems of the society. You need the courage to move on with what you perceive even when others around you tell you it won't materialize. To excel, you should not listen to the naysayers. Be inspired by the above famous people and others who followed their passions and succeeded. Passion is one of the most powerful ingredients for success.

105

You may sometimes feel that you will never make it; the above people could have felt the same way, but they persevered to create long-lasting legacies. Start small and begin your journey to success by making a positive impact in your community or industry. You might not have been born into riches, or your success may not always be spoon-fed but you can still make it big in life and create a lasting legacy. Whenever you feel turning your dreams into reality is impossible, remember that there are very many people some of whom are still living, who started small and made it big in their lives.

You can come from a humble beginning and excel so long as you work hard, commit to your ideas and take the necessary risks to see those ideas become reality. Draw inspirations from the massive successes who have come before you, and don't let your background, or lack of money or experience ever deter you from following your dreams. The above people found success because they saw needs that weren't being addressed, and addressed them using their gifts, skills and knowledge.

From a small beginning, they succeeded. Their backgrounds didn't limit them from pursuing their dreams. They knew they had something in them that could impact the world; they focused on it not their difficult conditions and background. They were visionary. Hailing from a great background is no guarantee that you will succeed in life. Likewise, originating from a simple background is not an indication that you will fail in life.

Every great achievement had a small beginning. The big tree you see today was once a seed, the cock that crows today was once an egg, even you, at some stage, were once an embryo in your mother's womb yet you grew up. Every big thing you see or can imagine, started small. Hidden in every small thing is a great seed which is in most cases invisible at the beginning. There is a seed of greatness in you. Have you discovered it? If so, then what are you doing with it? If not, then find out today.

It's your responsibility to nurture that seed so that it grows big and produces fruits. Small beginnings, when nurtured well, lead to great things. Small things, when managed well, eventually grow to become very big. Many people fail in life because they want to start big, forgetting that growth is a process that should never be rushed. When you start something on a small scale, but manage it well, it surely grows big. One of the keys to succeeding is management of the small things you have or do.

Most of those who fail in life focus on the big things they lack and ignore the small things they have. What you have, when you utilize it well, will bring you what you lack. The small things you have, when you take care of them, will bring you the big things you desire. Many people seek fortunes from outside yet their fortunes are within them. It's not what you lack but how you use what you have, that determines how successful you become in life.

What do you have? How do you use it? What seemingly small things are in your heart? Do it, and don't be surprised if you realize amazing results. Before looking for the things you lack, first make sure you are making the best use of the ones you have. At all times do not underrate the smallness of your deeds. Do not be afraid to embrace what you have. Do not compare what you have with what others have; copiously exploit what you have. Do not be afraid to step out in faith and try new things as you utilize what you have. The tenth verse of the sixteenth chapter of the book of Luke in the Holy Bible (NIV) contains these words: *"Whoever can be trusted with very little can also be trusted with much, and whoever is dishonest with very little will also be dishonest with much."*

Can you be trusted with very little? Are you honest with little? Please kindly answer the following questions honestly: How much is too little to you? How much is little to you? How much is neither little nor big to you? How much is big to you? And how much is too big to you?

To succeed, you have to be honest; you don't have to cheat to make it in life. If you keep a clean heart and righteous spirit and avoid disingenuousness as you gleefully practice honesty, love, truth, integrity, and justice in all your dealings and above all you rely fully on God, the small things you do and/or have will grow exponentially, into big things. As you prove yourself trustworthy with little, then you can be trusted with much.

Do wholeheartedly whatever task you have to do however small it might be. In the Holy Bible, Jesus Christ made a very powerful statement which is recorded in Matthew 13:31-32 (NIV) that, *"The kingdom of heaven is like a mustard seed, which a man took and planted in his field. Though it is the smallest of all your seeds, yet when it grows, it is the largest of garden plants and becomes a tree, so that the birds of the air come and perch in its branches."*

Hidden inside a mango is a seed which, when planted and managed properly, can grow and multiply into a forest of mango trees. Many people cannot foresee that forest-those who don't look and think beyond what they see physically. A seed may be very small or seemingly insignificant. However, plant that small seed with faith and manage it well, and it will grow, multiply and eventually provide comfort, haven, and rest for many others in which case it also makes way for you.

What is your "small" seed? What are you doing with it? Do you envision the big plant it can grow into? Small as your seed might be, don't despise it. Hold it in high regards because it will make way for you. Take on even the smallest tasks, and from them, you can realize great results. Seemingly insignificant beginnings do not restrict you from achieving great results. So take on the tasks that may seem to be small, and do them faithfully.

Develop the mindset with which you don't despise small things and beginnings. Our minds can wrongly limit us from achieving our dreams. Negative minded people always see nothing good in small things or beginnings. They are consequently limited by their situations through negative thinking. Strong-minded people are never restricted by the circumstances of their lives. They instead draw inspirations from their situations. The above people never allowed their circumstances to limit them in any way. They pursued their dreams and eventually realized them.

Do likewise; look beyond your current situation and start right away. That which for long you have wanted to start, start it immediately. Don't waste time waiting for what you think you need yet you have something to start with. Some people want to first get a lot of money to start something, not knowing that most of the richest people in the world today started with very little money which grew into what they have today. Do you wonder how they did it? Well, here is the secret: they managed the little very well. Management promotes growth and multiplication. If you don't manage something well, it will yield poor results if it doesn't die altogether. Whether a venture succeeds or fails lies in how it's managed. Whether you succeed or fail depends heavily on how you manage yourself.

Don't wait to first get a Ph.D. to start up something; some of the greatest achievers in the world never even went to school. However, if you have the opportunity to study, then get those papers and qualifications. You will surely need them. And the knowledge you will get from school will greatly help you to maximize your treasure. Start from where you are, with what is at your disposal. Don't wait to first become a pastor to embark on preaching the gospel; start today.

You don't have to first become an adult to in order to start doing something to transform the world. Remember that I started when I was a child. There are things you can start even though you are still a child; yet there are things you can start only when you are of age. The important thing is to discover what you have and maximize it. If you invest in waiting, you may wait till you die. That which you are waiting for may never come as you may need to use what you have to get what you want. You have to be wise; do not only work hard but also smart.

Many people lived and died poor because while they were alive, they kept on waiting and waiting till they breathed their last. They never laid hold of the small things they had. They wanted to start big; they consequently missed it. They died having achieved nothing apart from living miserable lives. Where are you in life? Do you see the great opportunities in the small things around you? Are you properly utilizing the resources you have or perhaps you are still procrastinating?

Are you waiting for someone, some moment or something to first come before you begin? Is it taking too long? Do you think you really need it in order to commence operation or you can begin with what is available to you right now? For how long will you wait? The truth is you might wait in vain. By the time you realize you were waiting for what perhaps you didn't even need at all, you will have wasted a lot of your precious time and consequently missed valuable opportunities.

However, this is not to suggest that you should rush while doing things. Remember the adage, "if you rush, you crush." You should not rush anything you do, let alone your progress in life. Don't start too early neither should you start too late; either way, you will miss it. Start at the right time. And never rush the growth of whatever you do. Don't use shortcuts otherwise; you will surely go off track. In life, you have to take the stairs and carefully climb to the top. There are important lessons to learn from each of the stairs both as you ascend and descend it.

You will learn to persevere, endure and be courageous. You will start small-from the very first one, and progress till you reach the top. That's the way to success. If you take the elevator-shortcuts, be sure to come back and hit yourself badly; you will only be fortunate not to die. Will you climb the stairs or take the elevator? For me, I am climbing the stairs; one by one I'm climbing them. I started small and I am progressing. The lessons from climbing the stairs are amazing.

I want to encourage you that where you are coming from does not determine where you are going. Irrespective of what you have, your background and/or family status and where you are right now, you too can start small and achieve big. Don't be discouraged by your conditions; be driven by them. With those very conditions of yours, with what you have, you can still succeed. If you don't see big opportunities in small things or beginnings, you will despise the small things or beginnings and may end up losing the big things and/or opportunities that are hidden in the small things or beginnings. You should therefore be vigilant.

Find the right environment for executing your activities and stay in it. Not every seed can grow in every place. There is the right place for every seed. Certain seeds thrive best in certain kinds of soil while other seeds cannot grow at all in particular soil types. Look for the right soil for your seed. Have the right people around you; those who will encourage but not discourage you. Invest heavily in yourself by focusing on improving your skills and experience as you pursue your dreams.

Without self-investment, it will be very difficult to beat the odds. Always focus on the future not the past; it holds the treasures that you desire. Don't be proud as that will only lead to your downfall. You will reap nothing from pride except failure. Use the challenges you encounter as stepping stones to your success. Even in the face of hardships, if you set your mind to turning your dreams into reality, you can make it. No matter how small your beginnings are, you can succeed in life. With a firm reliance on God, you can come into victory from even the most menacing beginning. The Holy Bible says in Zechariah 4:10 (NKJV) that, *"For who has despised the day of small things? For these seven rejoice to see the plumb line in the hand of Zerubbabel. They are the eyes of the LORD, which scan to and fro throughout the whole earth."*

Do not look down on the small things you have and do.

Don't undervalue simple beginnings or backgrounds. Be grateful for what you have; many people are praying to get it. Still many people have been praying for years to get where you are. Start small but with big dreams; you too can make it in life. Have a very clear and realistic vision for your life then you will properly utilize the opportunities you encounter in life.

CHAPTER TEN
CONQUER YOUR CHALLENGES

One day a man left his village and went to the bush to hunt. He had taken quite a long time without hunting as he had been sick. Hunting was his most revered way of life. He had been hunting since his childhood; he was introduced to it by his father who was known as the village's hunting hero as he would never go back home empty-handed when he went to the bush.

The man packed his tools and set off. As usual, he was hopeful as he walked through the thick forest surrounding the village, looking for wild animals to kill. However, his persistent efforts amounted to nothing that day as he never came across any animal that he could kill and take home. This experience was the first of its kind since he started hunting; just like his father, he too had never gone back home without at least an animal. He would sometimes kill more than one animal. This was a very unfortunate day for him and his family members who were definitely expecting him to go back home with at least an animal, which they could eat that day.

When the man was sick and could not go to hunt, a group of lions invaded the forest and were preying on the other animals. By the time he got well, the lions had eaten almost all the animals in the forest. Even most of the few that had survived had also fled the forest for their dear lives. The lions themselves were then starving as they would hardly find anything to feast on. The man therefore could not find animals to hunt as there was hardly any left that he could get and aim his hunting tools at. When dusk was approaching, he made up his mind to go back home as he could barely see clearly in the forest anymore. As for that day, his fate would be sealed in case he failed to land his eyes on an animal on his way back home; he and his family members could have nothing to eat.

Looking tired and frustrated, he started walking slowly to go back home. He was greatly shocked as he had never witnessed such a misfortune in his lifetime. He could not make anything out of the situation. He wondered what he would tell his family members when he reached home. Worse still, reaching home bare-handed would mean his exceptional reputation, of never going back home empty-handed, would have been smashed. He was therefore feeling very dissatisfied with what was happening. However, he quietly walked through the forest, while fully alert as he believed he could still find an animal to devour even at the last minute.

One of the lions in the forest had been scouting its prey in the forest the whole day yet had neither seen nor smelt any. The man had no idea about whatever was happening. He just continued walking, this time faster as the sun had almost disappeared. The hungry lion soon noticed that some trees were shaking unusually ahead of it, an indication that a prey could be within its vicinity. If that was the case, then at last it would have something to eat. Likewise, the man also saw trees shaking in front of him, where the lion was coming from, and quickly knew an animal could be around. This gave him some hope that he could finally find something to kill and take home. However, it was to be far from his expectations as it would be a matter of life and death for both him and the lion.

Both the man and the lion became keener and walked more carefully as they sought to discover whatever was shaking the trees ahead of them. The man stopped momentarily to strategically position himself so that he could at least catch a glimpse of what was ahead of him before he could confront it. The lion however, had already smelt the man and knew it had finally found a prey. What remained unclear to the lion was the size of the prey. The lion continued walking towards the man who had by this time, known that at least an animal was ahead of him. He was not moving as he sought to land his eyes on the animal.

Pretty soon he saw it from a distance even though not very clearly as it was already late and the animal was also at some good distance away from him. He thus hurriedly organized his hunting tools so as to face the animal. He removed his bow and arrows from his back, got his spear in one hand, tied his rope around his waist, prepared his sandals and got ready to start chasing the animal. The lion was increasing its speed as it got closer to its prey-the man.

The man also started moving very fast towards the lion with all his tools set. Faster he moved and very soon, he came face to face with the lion. Upon discovering that it was a lion, he immediately knew he was in an unimaginable danger as it was not even the least of what he expected. So he took to his heels and the hungry-and therefore-angry lion incessantly pursued him. He had never before encountered animals of the lion's caliber; this was therefore a disaster to him. He ran as fast as his legs could carry him, yet the lion continuously drew closer to him. The faster he ran, the closer it got to him. There was no one else in the forest at that time hence nobody could come to his rescue.

As he ran for his dear life, he threw away his hunting tools so as to enable him run faster; one by one he threw all of them. He even removed his sandals as he thought doing that would upsurge his speed. Yet still all those could not help him much, as the furious lion, which had traversed the forest since morning and caught nothing but had finally found its prey, was approaching him faster than he could ever imagine. The man reached a point where he was getting tired yet the lion was advancing even faster. He knew death was knocking on his door, but he would not surrender to it.

As he persistently ran, the lion became increasingly aggressive as it ran after him and could therefore soon catch him. He realized that it would be impossible to escape by just continuing to run as the lion was faster than him. To escape, he would have to do something different and urgently. He had thrown all his hunting tools as he ran through the forest. He could have done the obvious thing that is throwing his arrows, spears and the other tools at the lion. Unfortunately, that was not an option anymore as his tools were no longer at his disposal. He had to think of what to do so as to escape from the jaws of death that had engulfed him.

The lion was about to catch him when suddenly, a very powerful idea appeared on his mind. He swiftly stopped, turned to face the lion and started running aggressively towards it while roaring as loud as he could. The lion, upon seeing that the man had changed his direction and was now running belligerently towards it, stopped immediately and also changed its direction and started running even faster than before. The lion was greatly astonished as the prey it was previously chasing, had changed into something else and could therefore devour it.

The man ran after the lion while shouting at the top of his voice. Pretty soon, the lion ran and vanished in the forest. The man then, upon realizing that the lion had disappeared, took the road to his village and eventually made it home while running at breakneck speed through the forest. He reached home when he was exceptionally tired. He had encountered what as the first of its kind in his life. He had narrowly escaped being slain by the lion. It was the idea that came up on his mind, at the height of his challenge that made him survive.

What is the moral of this amazing story? How brave are you? How do you handle the challenges you encounter in life? Do you run away from them or you boldly face them? Do you perceive them to be indomitable or surmountable? Do you believe in yourself enough to face your challenges? Are you self-motivated to face the challenges that come your way or you only fully rely on other people to motivate you? Life is full of challenges, of different kinds. They are parts and parcels of life. We all encounter them quite often. How we handle them determines whether we overcome them or not.

The man in the story was embroiled in a very dangerous situation. The challenge before him could have cost him his dear life. If he had not been brave enough to face the lion, he would not have escaped. His immediate idea was to run away from the lion, something that would not be enough for him to escape as the lion was faster than him.

He was driven by fear that is why he decided to run away. However, in order to escape, he had to change his strategy. The idea that appeared on his mind later was for him to face the lion; perhaps it could flee. Left with almost nothing else to do as death was approaching faster than he could imagine, he decided to confront the lion. And behold the idea worked as the lion fled for its life for the prey had become more dangerous than the predator.

What challenges are you facing right now? What are you doing about them? Are you running away from them or confronting them? The main reason why some people overcome their challenges while others do not has to do with what they do about their challenges. In a nutshell, how they handle them. The difference between those who overcome their challenges and those who do not is that the latter run away from their challenges while the former confront them.

Running away from a problem is no solution to it; confront it and you will be able to solve it. No matter how fast you are, you will never overcome a challenge by running away from it; yet by facing it valiantly, you position yourself to subdue it. Sometimes you have to build your own confidence to face the problem at hand as there may be no one to help you just like the man in the story. Even when you are alone, press on. Don't rely too much on people. Sometimes you will find yourself alone in certain difficult situations. If you cannot motivate yourself to persevere, then you will hardly overcome those situations.

Many people, when faced with even the slightest difficulty, resort to crying and calling for help. They always believe other people have the solutions to their problems. They forget that they also have a role to play towards solving their problems. If there is no one to get them out of their problems, they eventually surrender to the problems and are very quick to tell other people that they failed to overcome the problems simply because there was no one to help them. The people you rely on will not always be there for you. They may not be available at the most critical time of your challenge. Relying on them therefore could make you surrender to your challenges in case they can't help you. Remember they also have their own challenges to overcome.

As you call people to help you when in a difficult situation, make sure you are also critically thinking of how you can overcome the situation in case they can't help you. They may not be able to offer you the required assistance as soon as you need it. You may just have to discover something hidden within you that could be what you need to go through the situation. An idea could appear on your mind at the height of the challenging situation that could get you out of it, just like the hunter in the story. The greatest idea normally comes at the most critical moment. Your mind is sharpest at the most crucial times of your trials; you just have to keep thinking.

However, at the same time be mentally flexible. Mental inflexibility will make it impossible for you to think of other ways to solve the problem. There could be many ways of solving a single problem but if you are mentally rigid, you will focus only on the ones you know or are familiar with. You will therefore fail to discover the other ways. Overcoming challenges requires you to think outside the box; that's where the solution could lie. If you are a person who only thinks within the box, then you won't be able to solve problems whose solutions are outside the box. Sometimes, in order to overcome the challenge at hand, you have to do the unusual thing just like the abrupt turning of the man which frightened the lion.

Always be strong-hearted even when death appears to be near. Never surrender to your challenges no matter how strong they appear to be; be brave and courageous as you face them. If you surrender, you will lose the battle. It is better to die fighting than to just sit and watch yourself being killed by your adversary. Overcoming challenges requires you to believe in yourself otherwise, it will always be hard for you to successfully navigate through the challenges you encounter in life. When faced with challenges, confront any fear that may arise, build your self-confidence and embrace the challenges; be hopeful, determined, persevering, brave, courageous, strong, self-motivated, and resilient, endure the pain and have faith in God. Never give up for any reason whatsoever, whenever in difficulties.

Challenges make us stronger; you will be much stronger after overcoming a challenge than you were before encountering it. Challenges teach us some of the most important lessons in life; we should therefore embrace them. You have to face your challenges to learn the lessons they offer. There is more to learn from life's trails than its triumphs.

Sometimes the only way to survive is to confront the problem otherwise it could subdue you. If the man had not been brave enough to confront the lion, he could never have survived. Your challenges are only as big as how you perceive them. How do you perceive the challenges you face? To some people, confronting the lion would be entirely impossible as they would never dare take that risk. Yet it's exactly what the man did in order to escape from the lion. You should be willing to do what it takes to overcome the challenges you are facing. You should discover that powerful idea that could save your life. Think differently from your usual ways. Be not timid but aggressive as you confront your challenges.

Don't run away from your challenges otherwise, they will appear bigger. In fact, the more you run away from your challenges, the bigger and stronger they become and the more scared you become and the higher your chances become of not overcoming them. Even a challenge as small as an orchid seed will scare you off if you shy away from it.

If you were the man in the story, what would you do in that situation? There is a lion you could be facing right now. What are you doing to overcome it? Are you crying as loud as you can yet nobody is responding? Are you running away from it or embracing it? Are you chasing it or it's chasing you? Do you think what you are doing right now will make you eventually overcome it? Are you acting out of fear or boldness? When you act out of fear, the results are always negative; but when you are driven by boldness, you attain positive results. What drives you when in difficult situations defines how you respond to such situations.

Therefore, you should examine yourself to discover what is currently driving you so that where necessary, you adjust accordingly. At first, the man in the story was being driven by fear, that's why he ran away from the ferocious lion. As he ran, he reassessed himself and upon realizing that he would not succeed that way, he changed his driving force to boldness. Under the auspices of boldness, he overcame the lion that had before appeared to be invincible to him. He realized he could chase it. The lion became smaller and smaller in his eyes as he ran after it. Maybe you have been struggling for so long to overcome a challenge.

Perhaps you feel you have already exhausted all your efforts yet with very little or no success at all. You might want to give up now. Yet the only thing you might need to do in order to overcome that 'stubborn' challenge is to simply change your strategy. You may have to just change your driving force and the results will be different. If you give up, you will surely not be able to overcome the challenge. Be conscious of your driving force as it determines how you respond to every situation in life. Dare yourself today and reposition yourself to face the challenge with a different perspective-that you can overcome it. Think and act differently and better this time. Do what you have never done before about the situation. You may not need the help of those you are over relying on. They might have greatly helped you previously yet they may not be able to help you this time. You therefore have to be wise.

You cannot overcome every challenge using the same approach. The approach that works with a particular challenge may not be feasible with another. If you persistently apply it, you will realize no positive result. Yet if you just stop and think deeply and discover the right approach and apply it, eventually you will overcome the challenge. Always be open-minded and flexible in life. That way, you won't be surpassed by whatever challenge comes your way irrespective of how big it might be.

Assuredly, you may never know the kind of challenge that might strike you in the next minute, hour or day; you just have to be at least mentally prepared to embrace whatever challenge you meet in life. Challenges will always come your way; they are prerequisites for success. If you really want to succeed, then you must first overcome them. It is not the challenge before you that matters most, but what you do about it. Do something different today about the challenges you are facing. Look at them from different angles. The solutions could lie in the angles you have never considered before.

Never surrender to your challenges. He who is hungry for success never gives in to difficulties. Never make giving up one of your options when faced with difficulties. Press on relentlessly. If you don't have a clear vision for doing something, then you will easily give up when you meet temptations along the way. Most of those who give up in life have no clear visions for their lives.

To have a vision is to have a clear picture of the end from the beginning. Therefore, before you start doing anything, make sure you envision its end from the beginning. Otherwise, you may give in to difficulties. Above all, always trust in, and rely on God; He will at all times be with you, fight for you and grant you victory over whatever trial you face. He is the only one you can rely on in every situation in life.

CONCLUSION

If a person does a great job, they deserve to be appreciated. Therefore, I sincerely thank you for reading the book up to this point. You have come to the end of the book. I strongly believe that you have enjoyed it. You have learnt feasible and practical time-tested techniques for discovering and ultimately utilizing the great treasure which lies inside you. I strongly believe that the book has guided you to discover and exploit your potential. I implore you to go ahead and apply what you have learnt so that you ultimately benefit from the book. Throughout the book, real-life stories were used to illustrate the techniques presented. It is my sincere hope that you learnt a lot from them.

Now that you have learnt how to tap your hidden treasure, you have to make a choice-whether to apply the techniques-in which case you will fully exploit the great treasure inside you, or not-in which case you will never fully tap your treasure; you will die and be buried with many undone things which you could have done. I challenge you never to go into the grave with anything undone, which you could have done. Endeavour to die empty.

I implore you to carefully apply the lessons and even go an extra mile by teaching others what you have learnt. It is only until you begin to teach others that you discover how much you know. The more you teach others, the more you learn and the better you become. Please note that if you carefully apply the techniques, you will surely get the desired results. I wrote this book to help you so that you discover and ultimately utilize your great treasure. Are you tapping your treasure right now? If yes, do you like what you are becoming? Do you realise how you are transforming lives? Can you see how you are making the world better than it is? Can you imagine how you will tremendously influence the world?

My heart will be filled with great joy to learn how the book has helped you. Kindly share with me your testimonies through my e-mail address below. Should you need any further assistance, then please do not hesitate to contact me at your convenience. I exhort you to recommend this book to other people and if possible, kindly put copies in their hands. To book me to speak at your events, use the e-mail address below. Finally, do not forget to get copies of my other books and read them; they will transform your life colossally. May God bless you immensely as you tap your hidden treasure ultimately.

Engineer Job Lazarus Okello
Motivational Speaker, Author, Mentor,
Researcher, Mechanical Engineer
and Entrepreneur.

131

E-mail: joblazaruslegend@gmail.com
Twitter: @Joblazlegend